WILLIAMS-SONOMA
COLLECTION

Pasta Soups
& Salads

WILLIAMS-SONOMA
COLLECTION

PASTA SOUPS & SALADS

GENERAL EDITOR
CHUCK WILLIAMS

RECIPES BY
JOANNE WEIR

PHOTOGRAPHY BY
JOYCE OUDKERK POOL

TIME
LIFE
BOOKS

Time-Life Books is a division of
Time-Life Incorporated

President and CEO: John Fahey, Jr.

TIME-LIFE BOOKS

President, Time-Life Books: John D. Hall
Vice President and Publisher: Terry Newell
Director of New Product Development: Regina Hall
Director of Financial Operations: J. Brian Birky
Editorial Director: Donia Ann Steele

All recipes include customary U.S. and metric measurements.
Metric conversions are based on a standard developed for this
book and have been rounded off. Actual weights may vary.
Unless otherwise stated, the recipes were designed for medium-
sized fruits and vegetables.

Cover: Spring Asparagus and Snap Pea Penne Salad (recipe on
page 68) is a flavorful example of a vegetable and pasta salad.

WILLIAMS-SONOMA
Founder: Chuck Williams

WELDON OWEN INC.
President: John Owen
Vice President and Publisher: Wendely Harvey
Managing Editor: Jill Fox
Recipe Analysis: Hill Nutrition Associates Inc.
    Lynne S. Hill, MS, RD; William A. Hill, MS, RD
Copy Editor: Carolyn Miller
Art Director: John Bull
Designer: Patty Hill
Production Director: Stephanie Sherman
Production Editor: Janique Gascoigne
Editorial Assistants: Stephani Grant, Marguerite Ozburn
Co-Editions Director: Derek Barton
Co-Editions Production Manager: Tarji Mickelson
Food Stylist: Susan Massey
Food Stylist Assistants: Andrea Lucich, Geri Lesko
Prop Stylist: Carol Hacker
Photographer's Assistant: Myriam Varela
Hand Model: Tracey Hughes
Indexer: ALTA Indexing Service
Proofreaders: Desne Border, Ken DellaPenta
Illustrator: Nicole Kaufman
Props Courtesy: Biordi, Pottery Barn, Williams-Sonoma
Special Thanks: Peggy Fallon, Mick Bagnato,
    Bryan's Meats, Cal-Mart

A Weldon Owen Production

First printing 1996
10 9 8 7 6 5 4 3 2 1

Library of Congress
Cataloging-in-Publication Data:

Weir, Joanne
    Pasta soups & salads / general editor,
    Chuck Williams ; recipes by Joanne Weir ;
    photography by Joyce Oudkerk Pool.
    p.   cm. — (Williams-Sonoma pasta collection)
    Includes index.
    ISBN 1-7835-0313-X
    1. Cookery (Pasta)   2. Soups.   3. Salads.
    I. Williams, Chuck.   II. Title.   III. Series.
    TXZ809.M17W45 1996b
    641.8'22 — dc20   95-31195
                                        CIP

The Williams-Sonoma Collection
conceived and produced by Weldon Owen Inc.
814 Montgomery Street, San Francisco, CA 94133

In collaboration with Williams-Sonoma
3250 Van Ness Avenue, San Francisco, CA 94109

Production by Mandarin Offset, Hong Kong
Printed in China

CONTENTS

Pasta Basics

THE PLEASURES OF PASTA

Of all the many guises in which pasta makes an appearance on our tables, soups and salads are among the most delightful. The pleasures of pasta soups and salads include high nutritional value, ease of preparation, ability to combine well with all types of foods and abundant ways in which they can be served. Pasta soups offer both heartiness and visual appeal. Using pasta as the foundation of a salad creates myriad possibilities for main courses or side dishes ideal for casual meals or elegant dining.

Use dried pasta for the recipes in this book. The various shapes should be available in most food stores. If a specific shape cannot be found, substituting a similarly sized pasta will not affect the dish. Fresh pasta can be substituted, as well, although an additional pleasure of dried pasta is its long shelf life, which allows you to make wonderful meals right from the pantry.

DRIED SEMOLINA PASTA

The recipes in this book were designed and tested using semolina pasta. Dried semolina pasta is high in dietary fiber, low in fat, cholesterol-free and contains generous amounts of protein, making it a beneficial part of a balanced diet. Unlike pasta made from white flour, dried semolina pasta has a sturdier consistency that helps it maintain its chewy texture when immersed in boiling liquids or coated with a dressing.

Dried semolina pasta is manufactured entirely from hard (durum in Latin) wheat, a variety high in the elastic substance known as gluten, which gives the pasta its desired sturdiness. Mixed with water, semolina flour forms a paste that is extruded through metal dies to make strands, ribbons, tubes or various other shapes (see pages 12–15). The pasta is then dried in chambers that carefully control humidity and temperature.

Look for dried semolina pasta on the shelves of well-stocked food markets, specialty foods stores and Italian delicatessens. By general consensus, imported Italian varieties are considered the best, but good varieties are now also being made outside of Italy; check labels, however, to make sure the pasta is made from 100 percent hard-wheat (semolina) flour.

Once you have opened the package, store all dried pasta in tightly covered glass containers in a cool, dark place. Use within a year.

NUTRITIONAL ANALYSIS

Each recipe in this book has been evaluated by a registered dietitian. The resulting analysis lists the nutrient breakdown per serving. Use these numbers to plan nutritionally balanced meals. All ingredients listed with each recipe have been included in the analysis. Exceptions are items inserted "to taste" and those listed as "optional."

When seasoning with salt, bear in mind that each teaspoon of regular salt contains 2,200 mg of sodium. The addition of black or white pepper does not alter nutrient values. Substituted ingredients, recipe variations and accompaniments suggested in the recipe introductions or shown in the photographs have not been included in the analysis.

NUTRITIONAL TERMS

CALORIES (KILOJOULES)
Calories provide a measure of the energy provided by any given food. A calorie equals the heat energy necessary to raise the temperature of 1 kg of water by 1° Celsius. One calorie is equal to 4.2 kilojoules—a term used instead of calories in some countries.

PROTEIN
One of the basic life-giving nutrients, protein helps build and repair body tissues and performs other essential functions. One gram of protein contains 4 calories. A healthy diet derives about 15 percent of daily calories from protein.

CARBOHYDRATES
Classed as either simple (sugars) or complex (starches), carbohydrates are the main source of dietary energy. One gram contains 4 calories. A healthy diet derives about 55 percent of daily calories from carbohydrates, with not more than 10 percent coming from sugars.

TOTAL FAT
This number measures the grams of fat per serving, with 1 gram of fat equivalent to 9 calories, more than twice the calories present in a gram of protein or carbohydrate. Experts recommend that total fat intake be limited to a maximum of 30 percent of total daily calories.

SATURATED FAT
Derived from animal products and some tropical oils, saturated fat has been found to raise blood cholesterol and should be limited to no more than one-third of total daily fat calories.

CHOLESTEROL
Cholesterol is a fatty substance present in foods of animal origin. Experts suggest a daily intake of no more than 300 mg. Plant foods contain no cholesterol.

SODIUM
Derived from salt and naturally present in many foods, sodium helps maintain a proper balance of body fluids. Excess intake can lead to high blood pressure, or hypertension, in sodium-sensitive people. Those not sensitive should limit daily intake to about 2,200 mg.

FIBER
Dietary fiber aids elimination and may help prevent heart disease, intestinal disease and some forms of cancer. A healthy diet should include 20–35 grams of fiber daily.

COOKING PERFECT PASTA

When cooking dried semolina pasta for use in soups or salads, follow the same general guidelines that apply to pasta cooked for any other culinary use. No special equipment—or culinary skill—is required. If you can boil water and tell time, you can cook perfect pasta.

It is customary to add salt to the boiling water prior to cooking pasta. For extra flavor use kosher salt, which is slightly coarser, is made without anti-caking additives and imparts more flavor than refined table salt. However, if a special need requires a sodium-free diet, the salt can be eliminated without an adverse effect on the finished dish.

EQUIPMENT NEEDS

For best results when cooking pasta, choose a two-handled pot large enough to allow the pasta to float freely while cooking. This will help prevent the pasta from sticking. Use a long-handled slotted spoon or cooking fork to stir the pasta. A pasta fork, also called a pasta puller, is a long-handled tool made of plastic or wood that looks like a flat spoon with teeth. It is handy for lifting long strands from the cooking pot and serving bowl. Thick pot holders or oven mitts and a sturdy colander that can withstand great heat are good investments in cooking pasta safely and successfully.

If you cook pasta frequently, consider a special pasta pot, which allows you to drain the pasta simply by lifting the insert from the pot, eliminating the need for pouring the pasta and its cooking water into a colander. Because the water is retained, a pasta pot is especially helpful when cooking a lot of pasta in batches.

AL DENTE DEFINED

The Italian phrase "al dente" has become a universally accepted term for perfectly cooked pasta. Simply translated, it means "to the tooth"—a slight resistance to the bite—aptly describing the desired tender but still chewy texture.

To test for doneness, use a long-handled slotted spoon, cooking fork or pasta puller to fish out a single piece or strand of pasta. Lift it from the boiling water a minute or so before the earliest suggested time for doneness.

Blow on the pasta briefly to cool it, then bite into it. The pasta should be tender but firm and chewy. It should not show any hard, white uncooked portion at its center; al dente does not mean underdone.

When pasta is added to a hot soup, it will continue to cook in the liquid. Cook soup pasta only until it is just al dente, so that it will better retain its distinctive texture in the finished dish.

COOKING PASTA: STEP-BY-STEP

1. BOILING THE WATER
Start with sufficient water in a large enough pot to allow the pasta to circulate freely. Over high heat, bring the water to a full, rolling boil. If desired, cover the pot to shorten the time needed to bring it to a boil.

2. ADDING SALT AND PASTA
When the water boils, add the salt. Do not add the salt before the water boils; doing so may cause an unpleasant aftertaste. When the water has returned to a boil, add the pasta, stirring to prevent it from sticking together.

3. BOILING THE PASTA
Cook the pasta, stirring occasionally, until it is al dente. Begin testing the pasta a minute or so before the earliest suggested time for doneness according to the recipes or the package directions.

4. DRAINING THE PASTA
Set a sturdy colander in the sink. Protecting your hands with pot holders or oven mitts, carefully lift the pot and pour its contents into the colander. Lift and shake the colander until all the water has drained from the pasta. Do not rinse the pasta.

5. DRESSING WITH OIL
Immediately transfer the pasta to a large bowl. For salads, drizzle the pasta with olive oil and toss to coat well. This will lightly season the pasta while preventing it from sticking together. Cool the oil-dressed pasta, uncovered, to room temperature. Covering the hot pasta may cause it to sour.

6. COOLING THE PASTA
Once cooled, cover and refrigerate the pasta for at least 1 hour and up to 24 hours prior to mixing with other ingredients. This provides time for the pasta to absorb the flavor of the oil. For most salads, allow the pasta to return to room temperature before serving.

PASTA FOR SOUPS

The kind of pasta suitable for soup should be a size and shape that enables you to pick it up with a soup spoon and eat it without the pasta slipping or slithering back into the bowl. Most of the pasta shapes shown opposite, along with any others of similar size or shape, will meet that criterion with ease; but even lengthy strands or ribbons of pasta may be used, provided you snap them into spoon-sized pieces before cooking.

In most cases, follow the instructions on pages 10–11 for cooking the pasta before adding it to the soup; take special care to cook the pasta only until the first moment that it is al dente, since it will continue cooking briefly in the hot soup. In some recipes, however, such as the Chicken and Farfalle Vegetable Soup on page 25, the pasta cooks right in the soup.

A PASTA SOUP MEAL

Discover the homey pleasure of serving soup as a main course with robust and filling pasta soups.

Pasta soups that also contain beans or lentils, such as Pasta, White Bean and Tomato Soup (recipe on page 33), are an especially good choice as a main course. This combination of grain and bean provides a well-balanced portion of protein and fiber while being lowfat and delicious. Remember that most of these soup recipe ingredients can be stored for many months in the pantry, making them ideal choices for emergency meals.

If you plan to serve one of the soups in this book as a main course, consider the quantity of each recipe as yielding 4 generous servings rather than the 6 first-course servings as designated. To serve more than 4, multiply the quantity as necessary.

For a satisfying meal, accompany a pasta soup with a mixed green salad, a crusty loaf of bread or home-baked quick bread, fresh fruit or another favorite dessert and your choice of beverage.

STORING PASTA SOUPS

One of the pleasures of making soup is the ease with which the quantity may be doubled or tripled, yielding extra soup to store in an airtight container in the refrigerator or freezer for future meals.

When making ahead one of the soups in this book, do not prepare the pasta in advance or add it to the soup before storage; prolonged immersion in liquid makes pasta mushy and causes it to disintegrate. Instead, prepare the soup without the pasta. Then, when reheating the soup, cook the pasta and add it to the soup just before serving.

ORECCHIETTE
Little Ears

12–15 minutes
cooking time

ELBOWS
7–10 minutes
cooking time

PENNE
Quills

10–12 minutes
cooking time

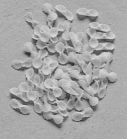

FARFALLINE
Little Butterflies

2–3 minutes
cooking time

FARFALLE
Butterflies

10–12 minutes
cooking time

TORTELLINI
Little Pies

10–12 minutes
cooking time for dried
4–5 minutes
cooking time for fresh

DITALINI
Little Thimbles

2–3 minutes
cooking time

STELLINE
Little Stars

2–3 minutes
cooking time

SMALL SHELLS
12–15 minutes
cooking time

PASTA FOR SALADS

Although ease of eating is not as critical a factor in the choice of pasta shapes for salad as it is for soup, it is still a matter for consideration. If you plan to serve the salad for an elegant occasion, you might want to select a pasta size or shape that can be eaten easily with a fork. Casual events allow for pasta salads that require the dexterous twirling of pasta strands or balancing of larger pasta shapes.

The other ingredients in the salad also play a factor in the choice of pasta you use. The sizes and shapes into which they are cut should be complemented by the size and shape of the pasta. Your choice of pasta can also add an element of wit to the salad: Witness the recipe on page 82, for example, in which pasta shells are the perfect choice for a salad featuring seafood.

Shown opposite are the pasta varieties used for the salads in this book. Feel free to substitute any other pastas of similar size or shape in any of the recipes.

SERVING PASTA SALADS

The introductory notes to the pasta recipes in this book offer useful ideas on the many roles they can play in a meal, from buffet or picnic food to side dish to main course. Quantities may easily be multiplied for larger gatherings, or halved for more intimate meals.

Note that in most cases the pasta, cooked in advance and chilled in the refrigerator, is tossed with the dressing and other ingredients shortly before serving. As the pasta will absorb the dressing and become softer over time, the salad, once tossed, is best if eaten within 24 hours.

PACKING PASTA SALADS

Perhaps the most traditional use of pasta salad is as a picnic food. Many of the salad recipes in this book lend themselves well to travel. Take any of the Vegetable Salad recipes (beginning on page 34), except those containing mayonnaise and any of the salads containing cooked chicken, lamb or beef. Storing seafood under less than ideal refrigeration is not recommended.

If you plan to serve one of the pasta salads at a picnic, it's a good idea to pack the chilled pasta, the dressing and the other salad ingredients in three separate containers, bringing along a large, lightweight serving container in which you can combine them once you've arrived at your destination. Use an ice chest or insulated bag and stack the salad containers between layers of ice. All perishable picnic foods should be stored at a temperature lower than 42°F (6°C).

LARGE SHELLS
12–15 minutes
cooking time

FARFALLE
Butterflies
10–12 minutes
cooking time

FUSILLI
Fuses
12–15 minutes
cooking time

LINGUINE
Small Tongues
5–8 minutes
cooking time

FETTUCCINE
Ribbons
7–10 minutes
cooking time

ORECCHIETTE
Little Ears
12–15 minutes
cooking time

RIGATONI
12–15 minutes
cooking time

ELBOWS
7–10 minutes
cooking time

TORTELLINI
Little Pies
10–12 minutes
cooking time for dried
4–5 minutes
cooking time for fresh

ORZO
Barley
5–8 minutes
cooking time

PENNE
Quills
10–12 minutes
cooking time

Pasta Soups

HERBED TOMATO, GARLIC AND MACARONI SOUP

Make this simple soup at the height of summer, when vine-ripened tomatoes are the most flavorful and fresh herbs are the most fragrant. If you're a real garlic lover, don't hesitate to double the quantity.

3 qt (3 l) water

2 teaspoons salt

4 oz (125 g) dried elbow pasta

2 tablespoons extra-virgin olive oil

1 small red (Spanish) onion, peeled and minced

¼ cup (1 oz/30 g) garlic cloves, peeled and minced

3 tomatoes, peeled and seeded *(see page 126)* or 3 cups (18 oz/560 g) chopped canned tomatoes

4 cups (32 fl oz/1 l) Chicken Stock *(recipe on page 127)*

1 tablespoon chopped fresh parsley

2 tablespoons chopped fresh chives

1½ teaspoons chopped fresh oregano

1½ teaspoons chopped fresh thyme

¼ teaspoon chopped fresh rosemary

1 tablespoon red wine vinegar
    Salt and freshly ground pepper

1. In a large pot over high heat, bring the water to a boil. Add the 2 teaspoons salt and the elbow pasta and cook according to the package directions or until al dente (see page 10), 7–10 minutes. Drain the pasta and toss it immediately with 1 tablespoon of the olive oil.

2. In a large pot over medium-low heat, warm the remaining 1 tablespoon olive oil. Add the onion and garlic and sauté slowly, stirring, until the onion is soft, about 10 minutes. Add the tomatoes, Chicken Stock, parsley, chives, oregano, thyme and rosemary and simmer for 20 minutes. Add the pasta, vinegar and salt and pepper to taste. Simmer until the pasta is heated through, about 2 minutes.

3. To serve, ladle into individual bowls.

Serves 6

NUTRITIONAL ANALYSIS: Calories 161 (Kilojoules 677); Protein 6 g; Carbohydrates 23 g; Total Fat 7 g; Saturated Fat 1 g; Cholesterol 0 mg; Sodium 153 mg; Dietary Fiber 2 g

PENNE AND SQUASH SOUP WITH SAGE CROUTONS

Smooth and creamy in texture, this substantial soup gains extra interest from cooked penne or other tube-shaped pasta stirred in just before serving. The aromatic, crunchy croutons make excellent use of day-old bread.

1   tablespoon plus 1 teaspoon extra-virgin olive oil

2   lb (1 kg) butternut squash, halved lengthwise and seeded

4   qt (4 l) water

2   teaspoons salt

6   oz (185 g) dried penne

1   tablespoon unsalted butter

3   bacon slices, coarsely chopped

1   large yellow onion, peeled and coarsely chopped

6   cups (48 fl oz/1.5 l) Chicken Stock *(recipe on page 127)*

    Freshly ground nutmeg

    Salt and freshly ground pepper

¾   cup (3 oz/90 g) coarsely shredded Gruyère cheese

18 whole flat-leaf (Italian) parsley leaves

SAGE CROUTONS

2   tablespoons extra-virgin olive oil

1   tablespoon finely chopped fresh sage or 2 teaspoons dried sage

    Salt and freshly ground pepper

8   oz (250 g) country-style bread, crust removed and cut into ¾-inch (2-cm) cubes

1. Prepare the Sage Croutons (see below).

2. Preheat an oven to 375°F (190°C).

3. Coat a baking sheet with the 1 teaspoon olive oil. Place the squash on the baking sheet cut-side down. Bake the squash until soft, about 1 hour. With a large spoon, scoop the squash pulp from the skin and discard the skin.

4. In a large pot over high heat, bring the water to a boil. Add the 2 teaspoons salt and the penne and cook according to the package directions or until al dente (see page 10), 10–12 minutes. Drain the penne and toss it immediately with the 1 tablespoon olive oil.

5. In a large pot over medium heat, melt the butter. Add the bacon and onion and cook, uncovered, until the onion is soft, about 10 minutes. Add the squash and Chicken Stock and simmer, uncovered, until the squash falls apart, about 30 minutes. Cool slightly. Transfer to the work bowl of a food processor fitted with the metal blade or a blender and purée. Return to the pot. Add the penne, nutmeg and salt and pepper to taste. Stir to mix well.

6. To serve, ladle into individual bowls and garnish with the Gruyère cheese, parsley and Sage Croutons.

SAGE CROUTONS

1. Preheat an oven to 350°F (180°C).

2. In a large bowl, combine the olive oil, sage and salt and pepper to taste. Add the bread cubes and toss to coat.

3. Place the bread cubes on a baking sheet and bake, tossing occasionally, until crisp and golden, 10–15 minutes.

Serves 6

NUTRITIONAL ANALYSIS: Calories 500 (Kilojoules 2,102); Protein 17 g; Carbohydrates 59 g; Total Fat 25 g; Saturated Fat 9 g; Cholesterol 28 mg; Sodium 543 mg; Dietary Fiber 5 g

PASTA IN BROTH WITH CHIVES

In Italy, this soup is called pasta in brodo. *It makes a wonderful first course. For added color and flavor, try adding green beans, fresh herbs, peas, Swiss chard (silverbeet) or spinach.*

2 lb (1 kg) chicken parts (necks and backs), fat removed

1 small onion, quartered

1 small carrot, peeled and coarsely chopped

⅛ teaspoon dried thyme

2 qt (64 fl oz/2 l) water

5 oz (155 g) dried soup pasta (stelline, ditalini or farfalline)

1 tablespoon minced fresh chives
   Salt and freshly ground pepper

½ cup (2 oz/60 g) grated Parmesan cheese

1. In a large pot over high heat, combine the chicken parts, onion, carrot, thyme and water and bring to a boil. Reduce the heat to low and simmer, uncovered, for 3 hours. Periodically add water to the pot to maintain the original level. Strain the broth and discard the bones. Skim the fat and discard.

2. In a large clean soup pot over medium-high heat, reheat the broth adding water, if necessary, to make 2 qt (64 fl oz/2 l). Add the pasta and cook according to the package directions or until al dente (see page 10), 2–3 minutes. Add the chives and salt and pepper to taste. Stir to mix well.

3. To serve, ladle into individual soup bowls and sprinkle with the Parmesan cheese. Serve hot.

Serves 6

NUTRITIONAL ANALYSIS: Calories 160 (Kilojoules 672); Protein 11 g; Carbohydrates 21 g; Total Fat 6 g; Saturated Fat 3 g; Cholesterol 6 mg; Sodium 305 mg; Dietary Fiber 1 g

CHICKEN AND FARFALLE VEGETABLE SOUP

You can use many different kinds of vegetables in this soup, selecting whatever is in season. Good options include asparagus, sugar snap peas, carrots and Swiss chard (silverbeet). Try other medium-sized pasta shapes in place of the farfalle.

1	small chicken (3 lb/1.5 kg), quartered and skin removed
2½	qt (2.5 l) water
1	large yellow onion, peeled and coarsely chopped
1	carrot, peeled and coarsely chopped
6	parsley sprigs
1	teaspoon finely chopped fresh thyme
2	bay leaves
3	celery stalks with leaves, trimmed and cut diagonally into ½-inch (12-mm) pieces
½	small head (6 oz/185 g) Savoy cabbage, coarsely chopped
8	oz (250 g) green beans, cut diagonally into 1-inch (2.5-cm) pieces
6	oz (185 g) dried farfalle
¼	cup (⅓ oz/10 g) finely chopped fresh parsley
1	tablespoon fresh lemon juice
	Salt and freshly ground pepper
¾	cup (3 oz/90 g) grated Parmesan cheese

1. In a large pot over high heat, combine the chicken, water, onion, carrot, parsley, thyme and bay leaves and bring to a boil. Reduce the heat to medium low and simmer, covered, until the chicken falls from the bone, about 1 hour.

2. Remove the chicken from the broth and cool. Strain the remaining broth and return it to the pot. Discard the vegetables. Remove the chicken from the bone and discard the bones. Tear the meat into 1-inch (2.5-cm) pieces and reserve the meat separately from the broth.

3. To the pot, add the celery, cabbage, green beans and farfalle and simmer, covered, until the farfalle is al dente (see page 10), 10–12 minutes. Add the chicken, parsley, lemon juice and salt and pepper to taste. Heat, stirring occasionally, until the chicken is warm.

4. To serve, ladle into individual bowls and top with the Parmesan cheese.

Serves 6

NUTRITIONAL ANALYSIS: Calories 319 (Kilojoules 1,342); Protein 33 g; Carbohydrates 29 g; Total Fat 8 g; Saturated Fat 3 g; Cholesterol 86 mg; Sodium 340 mg; Dietary Fiber 2 g

TORTELLINI AND ESCAROLE SOUP PARMESAN

Each rendition of this favorite Italian soup will vary with the type of tortellini or other small filled pasta used. Substitute spinach or Swiss chard (silverbeet) for the escarole, if desired.

6 cups (48 fl oz/1.5 l) Chicken Stock *(recipe on page 127)*
2 cups (16 fl oz/500 ml) water
8 oz (250 g) tortellini
1 small head escarole (6–8 oz/185–250 g)
Salt and freshly ground pepper
¾ cup (3 oz/90 g) grated Parmesan cheese

1. In a large pot over medium-high heat, bring the Chicken Stock and water to a boil. Immediately reduce the heat to medium, add the tortellini, cover and simmer according to the package directions or until al dente (see page 10), 10–12 minutes for dried, 4–5 minutes for fresh.
2. Cut the core end from the escarole. Remove the leaves from the head, rinse and dry well. Pile the leaves on top of one another and cut the escarole into ¼-inch (6-mm) strips.
3. To the pot, when the tortellini are al dente, add the escarole and salt and pepper to taste. Simmer, uncovered, until the escarole is soft, about 2 minutes.
4. To serve, ladle into individual bowls and garnish with the Parmesan cheese.

Serves 6

NUTRITIONAL ANALYSIS: Calories 202 (Kilojoules 850); Protein 14 g; Carbohydrates 22 g; Total Fat 9 g; Saturated Fat 4 g; Cholesterol 25 mg; Sodium 478 mg; Dietary Fiber 1 g

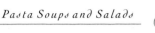

ITALIAN-STYLE CLAM SOUP WITH PASTA SHELLS

Serve this quick seafood soup with slices of toasted bread that you've rubbed with cut garlic cloves and spread with mayonnaise flavored with puréed garlic and a dash of cayenne. Or use the Sage Croutons on page 21.

3 qt (3 l) plus 2 cups (16 fl oz/500 ml) water

2 teaspoons salt

4 oz (125 g) dried small pasta shells

1 tablespoon extra-virgin olive oil

3 cups (24 fl oz/750 ml) Fish Stock *(recipe on page 127)*

1 cup (8 fl oz/250 ml) dry white wine

2 tomatoes, peeled, seeded and chopped *(see page 126)*, or 2 cups (12 oz/375 g) chopped canned tomatoes

4 garlic cloves, peeled and minced

6 parsley sprigs, tied together

½ teaspoon chopped fresh thyme

2 bay leaves
  Cayenne pepper

4 lb (2 kg) clams, scrubbed well

3 tablespoons finely chopped fresh parsley
  Salt and freshly ground pepper

1. In a large pot over high heat, bring the 3 qt (3 l) water to a boil. Add the 2 teaspoons salt and the pasta shells and cook according to the package directions or until al dente (see page 10), 12–15 minutes. Drain the pasta and toss it immediately with the olive oil.

2. In a large pot over high heat, combine the Fish Stock, wine, the 2 cups (16 fl oz/500 ml) water, tomatoes, garlic, parsley sprigs, thyme, bay leaves and cayenne to taste and bring to a boil. Reduce the heat to medium-low and simmer, covered, for 15 minutes. Remove and discard the parsley and bay leaves.

3. Discard any clams that do not close to the touch. Add the clams to the pot and simmer, covered, shaking the pot periodically, until they open, 3–5 minutes. Discard any unopened clams. Using a slotted spoon, remove the clams and let them cool slightly. Remove the clams from the shell and discard the shells.

4. Return the clams to the pot. Add the pasta, chopped parsley and salt and pepper to taste. Simmer until the pasta is heated through, about 1 minute.

5. To serve, ladle into individual bowls.

Serves 6

NUTRITIONAL ANALYSIS: Calories 173 (Kilojoules 728); Protein 9 g; Carbohydrates 21 g; Total Fat 3 g; Saturated Fat 0 g; Cholesterol 15 mg; Sodium 256 mg; Dietary Fiber 2 g

ONION BROTH WITH ORECCHIETTE

Onions, leeks, garlic and balsamic vinegar build a heady aroma in a light soup made hearty with ear-shaped orecchiette or other pasta shapes. Garnish the soup with garlic toasts.

1 tablespoon extra-virgin olive oil

4 oz (125 g) pancetta cut into ¼-inch (6-mm) dice

6 large yellow onions, peeled and thinly sliced

2 leeks, 2 inches (5 cm) of the green part and white part, thinly sliced

7 cups (56 fl oz/1.75 l) Chicken Stock *(recipe on page 127)*

6 oz (185 g) dried orecchiette

6 slices country-style bread

2 garlic cloves, peeled

3 tablespoons balsamic vinegar

   Salt and freshly ground pepper

1. In a large pot over medium heat, warm the olive oil. Add the pancetta, onions and leeks and sauté, stirring occasionally, until the onions and leeks are soft, about 15 minutes. Add the Chicken Stock and simmer, covered, for 15 minutes. Add the orecchiette and continue to simmer, covered, until the orecchiette is al dente (see page 10), 12–15 minutes.
2. To make the garlic toast, in a toaster or under a broiler (griller), toast the bread until golden. Rub the toast on one side with the garlic cloves.
3. To the pot, when the orecchiette is al dente, add the vinegar and salt and pepper to taste. Stir to mix well.
4. To serve, ladle into individual bowls and float 1 piece of garlic toast in each.

Serves 6

NUTRITIONAL ANALYSIS: Calories 407 (Kilojoules 1710); Protein 16 g; Carbohydrates 63 g; Total Fat 13 g; Saturated Fat 4 g; Cholesterol 11 mg; Sodium 522 mg; Dietary Fiber 6 g

PASTA, WHITE BEAN AND TOMATO SOUP

A variation on a signature soup of Tuscany called pasta e fagioli, *this recipe includes more tomatoes and pasta. Warming the rosemary garnish in olive oil releases its distinctive fragrance.*

1 cup (7 oz/220 g) dried small white (navy) beans

4 tablespoons (2 fl oz/60 ml) extra-virgin olive oil

1 onion, peeled and finely chopped

3 garlic cloves, peeled and minced

3 tomatoes, peeled and seeded *(see page 126)* or 3 cups (18 oz/560 g) chopped canned tomatoes

Salt and freshly ground pepper

5 cups (40 fl oz/1.25 l) Chicken Stock, Vegetable Stock *(recipes on pages 126–127)* or water

1 tablespoon finely chopped fresh rosemary

5 oz (155 g) dried elbow pasta

1. Rinse the beans; remove and discard any stones or damaged beans. Place in a bowl, add water to cover and soak for about 3 hours.

2. Drain the beans and place in a saucepan over high heat with water to cover by 2 inches (5 cm). Bring to a boil, reduce the heat to low and simmer gently, uncovered, until the skins begin to split and the beans are tender, 45–60 minutes. Drain and set aside.

3. In a large pot over medium-low heat, warm 2 tablespoons of the olive oil. Add the onion and garlic and sauté slowly, stirring, until the onion is soft, about 10 minutes. Add the tomatoes and salt and pepper to taste and simmer for 20 minutes. Add the Chicken or Vegetable Stock or water and simmer, covered, for 20 minutes. Add the beans and simmer, covered, for 20 minutes.

4. In a small saucepan over medium heat, warm the remaining 2 tablespoons olive oil. Add the rosemary and immediately remove the pan from the heat. Reserve, at room temperature, until serving.

5. To the pot, add the pasta and simmer until it is al dente (see page 10), 12–15 minutes.

6. To serve, ladle into individual bowls and drizzle with the rosemary mixture.

Serves 6

NUTRITIONAL ANALYSIS: Calories 331 (Kilojoules 1390); Protein 14 g; Carbohydrates 47 g; Total Fat 13 g; Saturated Fat 2 g; Cholesterol 0 mg; Sodium 109 mg; Dietary Fiber 6 g

Vegetable Salads

FARFALLE SALAD WITH SMOKED MOZZARELLA

The classic combination of mozzarella, tomatoes and basil gains new distinction by using a smoked version of the cheese. Serve with toasted bread topped with butter and sprinkled with herbs.

5	qt (5 l) water
1	tablespoon salt
12	oz (375 g) dried farfalle
5	tablespoons (3 fl oz/80 ml) extra-virgin olive oil
2	tablespoons balsamic vinegar
	Salt and freshly ground pepper
1¼	cups (5 oz/155 g) coarsely shredded smoked mozzarella cheese
18	cherry tomatoes, halved
1	cup (1 oz/30 g) packed fresh basil leaves

1. In a large pot over high heat, bring the water to a boil. Add the 1 tablespoon salt and the farfalle and cook according to the package directions or until al dente (see page 10), 10–12 minutes. Drain the farfalle and toss it immediately with 1 tablespoon of the olive oil. Cover and cool completely in the refrigerator, 1–24 hours.

2. In a large bowl, whisk together the remaining 4 tablespoons (2 fl oz/60 ml) olive oil, vinegar and salt and pepper to taste. Add the farfalle, mozzarella cheese, tomatoes and basil. Toss to mix well.

3. To serve, place in a serving bowl or divide among individual plates. Serve at room temperature.

Serves 6

NUTRITIONAL ANALYSIS: Calories 397 (Kilojoules 1,669); Protein 12 g; Carbohydrates 49 g; Total Fat 18 g; Saturated Fat 5 g; Cholesterol 18 mg; Sodium 289 mg; Dietary Fiber 3 g

ORECCHIETTE AND WINTER FRUIT SALAD

Pears and pecans may be substituted for apples and walnuts in this version of the classic Waldorf salad, an old American favorite, traditionally made without pasta. Here, the orecchiette provides a heartiness that makes this salad a meal.

5   qt (5 l) water

1   tablespoon salt

12   oz (375 g) dried orecchiette

1   tablespoon olive oil

⅔   cup (5 fl oz/160 ml) bottled mayonnaise

1   tablespoon fresh lemon juice
     Salt and freshly ground pepper

1   celery stalk with leaves, cut into ¼-inch (6-mm) slices

2   ripe green apples, peeled, cored and diced

36   seedless red grapes, halved

¾   cup (3 oz/90 g) walnuts, toasted *(see page 124)*

1. In a large pot over high heat, bring the water to a boil. Add the 1 tablespoon salt and the orecchiette and cook according to the package directions or until al dente (see page 10), 10–12 minutes. Drain the orecchiette and toss it immediately with the olive oil. Cover and cool completely in the refrigerator, 1–24 hours.

2. In a large bowl, combine the mayonnaise, lemon juice and salt and pepper to taste. Whisk to mix well.

3. Add the orecchiette, celery, apples, grapes and walnuts. Toss to mix well.

4. To serve, place in a serving bowl or divide among individual plates. Serve cold.

Serves 6

NUTRITIONAL ANALYSIS: Calories 543 (Kilojoules 2,281); Protein 10 g; Carbohydrates 59 g; Total Fat 32 g; Saturated Fat 4 g; Cholesterol 14 mg; Sodium 341 mg; Dietary Fiber 4 g

ORZO AND VEGETABLE CONFETTI SALAD

With its wide assortment of finely diced vegetables and chopped herbs, this salad does look like a celebration. For a more zesty dressing, use a lemon-flavored oil in place of the plain olive oil. Serve with grilled chicken.

2   qt (2 l) water

2   tablespoons salt

1½   cups (11 oz/345 g) orzo

5   tablespoons (3 fl oz/80 ml) extra-virgin olive oil

1   teaspoon grated lemon zest

⅓   cup (3 fl oz/80 ml) fresh lemon juice

    Salt and freshly ground pepper

12   radishes, diced

3   carrots, peeled and diced

8   green (spring) onions, green and white parts, thinly sliced

¼   cup (2 oz/10 g) capers, drained

¼   cup (⅓ oz/10 g) finely chopped fresh chives

2   tablespoons finely chopped fresh parsley

1   lemon, cut into 6 slices

1. In a large pot over high heat, bring the water to a boil. Add the 2 tablespoons salt and the orzo and cook until tender, 5–8 minutes. Drain the orzo and immediately toss it with 1 tablespoon of the olive oil. Cover and cool completely in the refrigerator, 1–24 hours.

2. In a large bowl, whisk together the remaining 4 tablespoons olive oil, lemon zest, lemon juice and salt and pepper to taste. Add the radishes, carrots, green onions, capers, chives, parsley and orzo. Toss to mix well.

3. To serve, place in a serving bowl or divide among individual plates and garnish with the lemon slices. Serve at room temperature.

Serves 6

NUTRITIONAL ANALYSIS: Calories 323 (Kilojoules 1,358); Protein 8 g; Carbohydrates 47 g; Total Fat 13 g; Saturated Fat 2 g; Cholesterol 0 mg; Sodium 524 mg; Dietary Fiber 3 g

FARFALLE SALAD WITH CAESAR DRESSING

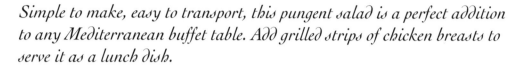

Simple to make, easy to transport, this pungent salad is a perfect addition to any Mediterranean buffet table. Add grilled strips of chicken breasts to serve it as a lunch dish.

5   qt (5 l) water

2   teaspoons salt

12 oz (375 g) dried farfalle

1   tablespoon plus ¼ cup (2 fl oz/ 60 ml) extra-virgin olive oil

¼   lb country-style bread, crust removed, cut into ¾-inch (2-cm) cubes

3   cloves garlic, peeled and minced
    Salt and freshly ground pepper

½   cup (2 oz/60 g) grated Parmesan cheese

CAESAR DRESSING

2   cloves garlic, peeled and minced

2   teaspoons Dijon-style mustard

2   tablespoons fresh lemon juice

4   anchovy fillets in olive oil, drained and mashed

½   cup (4 fl oz/125 ml) bottled mayonnaise

¼   cup (2 fl oz/60 ml) extra-virgin olive oil

¼   cup (2 fl oz/60 ml) heavy (double) cream

1. Preheat an oven to 350°F (180°C).

2. In a large pot over high heat, bring the water to a boil. Add the 2 teaspoons salt and the farfalle and cook according to the package directions or until al dente (see page 10), 10–12 minutes. Drain the farfalle and toss it immediately with the 1 tablespoon olive oil. Cover and cool completely in the refrigerator, 1–24 hours.

3. Prepare the Caesar Dressing (see below).

4. To make the croutons, toss the bread with the ¼ cup (2 fl oz/60 ml) olive oil, garlic and salt and pepper to taste. Place on a baking sheet and bake, tossing with a spatula occasionally, until golden and crisp, 10–15 minutes.

5. To serve, place the farfalle in a serving bowl or divide among individual plates. Add the Caesar Dressing and salt and pepper to taste. Toss to mix well. Garnish with the croutons and Parmesan cheese. Serve at room temperature.

CAESAR DRESSING

1. In a large bowl, whisk together the garlic, mustard, lemon juice, anchovies and mayonnaise. In a slow, steady stream, whisk in the oil, then gradually stir in the cream.

Serves 6

NUTRITIONAL ANALYSIS: Calories 651 (Kilojoules 2,734); Protein 13 g; Carbohydrates 55 g; Total Fat 43 g; Saturated Fat 9 g; Cholesterol 32 mg; Sodium 691 mg; Dietary Fiber 3 g

ELBOW PASTA AND SPINACH SALAD

Simple ingredients form lively contrasts of color, texture and flavor in this healthy salad. Pecans or hazelnuts (filberts) can be substituted for the walnuts. Add radicchio for still more color.

5   qt (5 l) water
1   tablespoon salt
12 oz (375 g) dried large elbow pasta
6   tablespoons (4 fl oz/125 ml) extra-virgin olive oil
2   shallots, peeled and minced
3   tablespoons sherry vinegar
1   tablespoon Dijon-style mustard
    Salt and freshly ground pepper
8   oz (250 g) spinach, stemmed and cut into ½-inch (12-mm) strips
¾   cup (3 oz/90 g) shelled walnuts, toasted *(see page 124)*
3   oz (90 g) Gruyère cheese, sliced

1. In a large pot over high heat, bring the water to a boil. Add the 1 tablespoon salt and the elbow pasta and cook according to the package directions or until al dente (see page 10), 7–10 minutes. Drain the pasta and toss it immediately with 1 tablespoon of the olive oil. Cover and cool completely in the refrigerator, 1–24 hours.
2. In a large bowl, whisk together the shallots, vinegar, mustard, the remaining 5 tablespoons (3 fl oz/80 ml) olive oil and salt and pepper to taste. Add the pasta, spinach and walnuts. Toss to mix well.
3. To serve, place in a serving bowl or divide among individual plates. Top with the Gruyère cheese. Serve at room temperature.

Serves 6

NUTRITIONAL ANALYSIS: Calories 491 (Kilojoules 2,064); Protein 14 g; Carbohydrates 48 g; Total Fat 28 g; Saturated Fat 5 g; Cholesterol 16 mg; Sodium 325 mg; Dietary Fiber 3 g

BROKEN FETTUCCINE SALAD WITH RADICCHIO

Breaking dried fettuccine into bite-sized lengths makes them easier to eat in a salad. You can substitute linguine or other pasta ribbons, if you like. Serve as a first course, or add thin strips of grilled chicken breast for a light main dish.

6 qt (6 l) water

1 tablespoon salt

1 lb (500 g) dried fettuccine, broken into 2-inch (5-cm) pieces

4 tablespoons (2 fl oz/60 ml) extra-virgin olive oil

1 small head radicchio (6–8 oz/ 185–250 g)

2 tablespoons red wine vinegar

4 oz (125 g) Gorgonzola cheese, cut into small pieces

¼ cup (2 fl oz/60 ml) heavy (double) cream

¼ cup (2 fl oz/60 ml) plain yogurt
    Salt and freshly ground pepper

½ cup (2½ oz/75 g) pecans, toasted *(see page 124)*

1. In a large pot over high heat, bring the water to a boil. Add the 1 tablespoon salt and the fettuccine and cook according to the package directions or until al dente (see page 10), 7–10 minutes. Drain the fettuccine and toss it immediately with 1 tablespoon of the olive oil. Cover and cool completely in the refrigerator, 1–24 hours.

2. Cut the core from the radicchio. Remove the leaves from the head, rinse and dry well. Pile the leaves on top of one another and cut the radicchio into ¼-inch (6-mm) strips. Set aside.

3. To make the dressing, in the work bowl of a food processor fitted with the metal blade or a blender, combine the remaining 3 tablespoons olive oil, vinegar, Gorgonzola cheese, cream, yogurt and salt and pepper to taste. Pulse until smooth.

4. In a large bowl, combine the fettuccine and dressing. Toss to mix well. Add the radicchio and pecans and toss gently.

5. To serve, place in a serving bowl or divide among individual plates. Serve at room temperature.

Serves 6

NUTRITIONAL ANALYSIS: Calories 542 (Kilojoules 2,278); Protein 18 g; Carbohydrates 58 g; Total Fat 29 g; Saturated Fat 10 g; Cholesterol 103 mg; Sodium 546 mg; Dietary Fiber 4 g

$\mathcal{S}$PICY FUSILLI WITH BROCCOLI AND CAULIFLOWER SALAD

In Italy, broccoli and cauliflower are often served together, showing off their complementary flavors and contrasting colors. Serve with breaded veal scallopini.

5   qt (5 l) water
1   tablespoon salt
12 oz (375 g) dried fusilli
6   tablespoons (3 fl oz/90 ml) extra-virgin olive oil
5   cups (10 oz/300 g) broccoli florets
5   cups (10 oz/300 g) cauliflower florets
6   tablespoons fresh lemon juice
6   anchovy fillets in olive oil, drained and mashed
3   garlic cloves, peeled and minced
¼ teaspoon red pepper flakes
    Fresh chives

1. In a large pot over high heat, bring the water to a boil. Add the 1 tablespoon salt and the fusilli and cook according to the package directions or until al dente (see page 10), 12–15 minutes. Drain the fusilli and toss it immediately with 1 tablespoon of the olive oil. Cover and cool completely in the refrigerator, 1–24 hours.
2. In a large pot of boiling salted water over high heat, cook the broccoli and cauliflower until tender, 2–4 minutes. Drain and cool completely in the refrigerator.
3. In a large bowl, whisk together the remaining 5 tablespoons (3 fl oz/80 ml) olive oil, lemon juice, anchovies, garlic and red pepper flakes. Add the fusilli, broccoli and cauliflower. Toss to mix well.
4. To serve, divide among individual plates. Garnish with the chives. Serve at room temperature.

Serves 6

NUTRITIONAL ANALYSIS: Calories 369 (Kilojoules 1,550); Protein 11 g; Carbohydrates 51 g; Total Fat 16 g; Saturated Fat 2 g; Cholesterol 2 mg; Sodium 358 mg; Dietary Fiber 5 g

MINTY ORZO, LENTIL AND FETA SALAD

Rice-shaped orzo pasta contrasts delightfully with the similar-sized lentils in a Mediterranean-inspired salad that makes a good companion to grilled lamb chops for warm-weather entertaining.

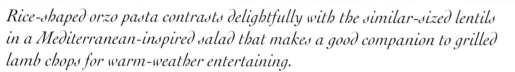

6 cups (48 fl oz/1.5 l) water

1 tablespoon salt

1¼ cups (9 oz/280 g) orzo

6 tablespoons (3 fl oz/90 ml) extra-virgin olive oil

¾ cup (5 oz/155 g) brown lentils

¼ cup (2 fl oz/60 ml) red wine vinegar

3 garlic cloves, peeled and minced
Salt and freshly ground pepper

½ cup (¾ oz/20 g) finely chopped fresh mint

½ cup (¾ oz/20 g) finely chopped fresh dill

1 small red (Spanish) onion, peeled and diced

10 oz (315 g) feta cheese, crumbled

¾ cup (4 oz/125 g) Kalamata olives, pitted and coarsely chopped

6 fresh mint or dill sprigs

1. In a large saucepan over high heat, bring the water to a boil. Add the 1 tablespoon salt and the orzo and cook until tender, 5–8 minutes. Drain the orzo and toss it immediately with 1 tablespoon of the olive oil. Cover and cool completely in the refrigerator, 1–24 hours.

2. Rinse the lentils; remove and discard any stones or damaged lentils. Drain and place in a saucepan over high heat with water to cover by 2 inches (60 cm). Bring to a boil, reduce the heat to low and simmer, uncovered, until tender, 15–20 minutes. Drain immediately and set aside to cool.

3. In a large bowl, whisk together the remaining 5 tablespoons (3 fl oz/80 ml) olive oil, vinegar, garlic and salt and pepper to taste. Add the orzo, lentils, chopped mint and dill, onion, feta cheese and olives. Toss to mix well.

4. To serve, place in a serving bowl or divide among individual plates and garnish with the herb sprigs. Serve at room temperature.

Serves 6

NUTRITIONAL ANALYSIS: Calories 563 (Kilojoules 2,363); Protein 20 g; Carbohydrates 52 g; Total Fat 32 g; Saturated Fat 10 g; Cholesterol 42 mg; Sodium 1,304 mg; Dietary Fiber 4 g

CATALONIAN RIGATONI SALAD

Romesco, a boldly flavored sauce from the Spanish province of Catalonia, inspired the dressing for this simple salad of rigatoni or other medium-sized tubes. For a more substantial dish, add steamed mussels.

5   qt (5 l) water

1   tablespoon salt

12 oz (375 g) dried rigatoni

5   tablespoons (3 fl oz/80 ml) extra-
    virgin olive oil

1   slice coarse-textured white bread,
    halved

¼   cup (1 oz/30 g) blanched almonds

1   tomato, peeled and seeded *(see page
    126)*, or 1 cup (6 oz/185 g) chopped
    canned tomatoes

2   garlic cloves, peeled and minced

2   teaspoons sweet paprika

¼   teaspoon red pepper flakes

3   tablespoons sherry vinegar
    Salt and freshly ground pepper

3   red bell peppers (capsicums),
    roasted, peeled, stemmed, seeded,
    deribbed and diced *(see page 125)*

¼   cup (⅓ oz/10 g) coarsely chopped
    fresh parsley

1. In a large pot over high heat, bring the water to a boil. Add the 1 tablespoon salt and the rigatoni and cook according to the package directions or until al dente (see page 10), 12–15 minutes. Drain the rigatoni and toss it immediately with 1 tablespoon of the olive oil. Cover and cool completely in the refrigerator, 1–24 hours.

2. To make the dressing, in a frying pan over medium heat, heat 1 tablespoon of the olive oil. Add the bread and fry, turning occasionally, until golden on both sides, about 2 minutes. Using a slotted spoon, transfer the bread to the work bowl of a food processor fitted with the metal blade or a blender. In the same pan over medium heat, toast the almonds, until golden, about 2 minutes. Add the almonds, tomatoes, garlic, paprika and red pepper flakes to the food processor or blender and pulse several times. In a measuring cup, combine the vinegar and the remaining 3 tablespoons olive oil. With the motor running, pour the olive oil mixture in a steady stream into the work bowl. Add salt and pepper to taste. Cover and set aside for 1 hour before using.

3. In a large bowl, combine the rigatoni, dressing, peppers and parsley. Toss to mix well.

4. To serve, place in a serving bowl or divide among individual plates. Serve at room temperature.

Serves 6

NUTRITIONAL ANALYSIS: Calories 371 (Kilojoules 1,556); Protein 9 g; Carbohydrates 52 g; Total Fat 16 g; Saturated Fat 2 g; Cholesterol 0 mg; Sodium 221 mg; Dietary Fiber 4 g

CHEESE TORTELLINI SALAD WITH PESTO DRESSING

Many food stores and delicatessens carry dried or freshly made tortellini in a mixture of different colored and flavored doughs: plain egg dough, green spinach and red tomato, which would add color and flavor to this simple salad.

5 qt (5 l) water

1 tablespoon salt

12 oz (375 g) cheese tortellini

5 tablespoons (3 fl oz/80 ml) extra-virgin olive oil

1 cup (1½ oz/45 g) packed fresh basil leaves

3 tablespoons pine nuts

3 garlic cloves, peeled and minced

½ cup (2 oz/60 g) grated Parmesan cheese

Salt and freshly ground pepper

1. In a large pot over high heat, bring the water to a boil. Add the 1 tablespoon salt and the tortellini and cook according to the package directions or until al dente (see page 10), 10–12 minutes for dried, 4–5 minutes for fresh. Drain the tortellini and toss it immediately with 1 tablespoon of the olive oil. Cover and cool completely in the refrigerator, 1–24 hours.

2. To make the pesto dressing, in the work bowl of a food processor fitted with the metal blade or a blender, combine the basil, pine nuts, garlic, the remaining 4 tablespoons (2 fl oz/60 ml) olive oil and one half of the Parmesan cheese. Process at high speed for 1 minute. Stop, scrape down the sides of the work bowl and continue to process until smooth. Add the remaining Parmesan cheese and pulse a few times to combine. Add salt and pepper to taste.

3. In a large bowl, combine the tortellini and pesto dressing. Toss to mix well.

4. To serve, place in a serving bowl or divide among individual plates. Serve at room temperature.

Serves 6

NUTRITIONAL ANALYSIS: Calories 343 (Kilojoules 1,442); Protein 12 g; Carbohydrates 31 g; Total Fat 20 g; Saturated Fat 5 g; Cholesterol 30 mg; Sodium 540 mg; Dietary Fiber 1 g

PENNE SALAD WITH PEPPERS AND TOMATOES

A colorful confetti of summertime vegetables enlivens penne or other thin, tube-shaped pasta, served here as a side dish to grilled halibut. Yellow bell peppers provide a sweeter flavor than the green versions.

5 qt (5 l) water
1 tablespoon salt
12 oz (375 g) dried penne
6 tablespoons (3 fl oz/90 ml) extra-virgin olive oil
6 tablespoons (3 fl oz/90 ml) fresh lemon juice
3 garlic cloves, peeled and minced
1 jalapeño pepper, seeded and minced
1 teaspoon ground cumin
3 yellow bell peppers (capsicums), roasted, peeled, stemmed, seeded, deribbed and diced *(see page 125)*
4 large ripe tomatoes, peeled, seeded and diced *(see page 126)*
1 large cucumber, peeled, seeded and diced
½ cup (¾ oz/20 g) finely chopped cilantro (fresh coriander)

1. In a large pot over high heat, bring the water to a boil. Add the 1 tablespoon salt and the penne and cook according to the package directions or until al dente (see page 10), 10–15 minutes. Drain the penne and toss it immediately with 1 tablespoon of the olive oil. Cover and cool completely in the refrigerator, 1–24 hours.

2. In a large bowl, whisk together the remaining 5 tablespoons (3 fl oz/80 ml) olive oil, lemon juice, garlic, jalapeño and cumin. Add the penne, peppers, tomatoes, cucumber and cilantro. Toss to mix well.

3. To serve, place in a serving bowl or divide among individual plates. Serve at room temperature.

Serves 6

NUTRITIONAL ANALYSIS: Calories 384 (Kilojoules 1,614); Protein 9 g; Carbohydrates 56 g; Total Fat 16 g; Saturated Fat 2 g; Cholesterol 0 mg; Sodium 212 mg; Dietary Fiber 5 g

RIGATONI SALAD WITH ARTICHOKE HEARTS

Other medium-sized pasta tubes would also go well with the quartered artichoke hearts. When artichokes are in season, try making the salad with freshly cooked artichoke hearts. Frozen ones will work as well.

5 qt (5 l) water

1 tablespoon salt

12 oz (375 g) dried rigatoni

6 tablespoons (3 fl oz/90 ml) extra-virgin olive oil

3 tablespoons fresh lemon juice

3 garlic cloves, peeled and minced

1 tablespoon finely chopped fresh oregano

Salt and freshly ground pepper

18 artichoke hearts bottled in olive oil, drained and cut into quarters

3 tablespoons finely chopped fresh parsley

3 oz (90 g) Parmesan cheese

1 lemon, cut into 6 wedges

1. In a large pot over high heat, bring the water to a boil. Add the 1 tablespoon salt and the rigatoni and cook according to the package directions or until al dente (see page 10), 12–15 minutes. Drain the rigatoni and toss it immediately with 1 tablespoon of the olive oil. Cover and cool completely in the refrigerator, 1–24 hours.

2. In a large bowl, whisk together the remaining 5 tablespoons (3 fl oz/80 ml) olive oil, lemon juice, garlic, oregano and salt and pepper to taste. Add the artichoke hearts, rigatoni and parsley. Toss to mix well.

3. To serve, place in a serving bowl or divide among individual plates. Using a cheese grater or shredder, grate the Parmesan cheese over the salad. Garnish with the lemon wedges. Serve at room temperature.

Serves 6

NUTRITIONAL ANALYSIS: Calories 369 (Kilojoules 1,549); Protein 16 g; Carbohydrates 57 g; Total Fat 10 g; Saturated Fat 3 g; Cholesterol 11 mg; Sodium 459 mg; Dietary Fiber 4 g

CUMIN ORECCHIETTE AND CHICK-PEA SALAD

With the chick-peas and pasta providing a balanced source of protein, this salad makes an excellent vegetarian main course. In place of the chick-peas, use cannellini, small white (navy), black or pinto beans.

1 cup (7 oz/220 g) dried chick-peas (garbanzo beans)

5 qt (5 l) water

1 tablespoon salt

12 oz (375 g) dried orecchiette

6 tablespoons (3 fl oz/90 ml) extra-virgin olive oil

3 tablespoons red wine vinegar

2 tablespoons tomato paste

3 garlic cloves, peeled and minced

2 teaspoons ground cumin
Salt and freshly ground pepper

¼ cup (⅓ oz/10 g) sliced fresh mint
Fresh mint sprigs

1. Rinse the chick-peas; remove and discard any stones or damaged peas. In a large bowl, combine the chick-peas and plenty of water to cover and soak for about 3 hours.
2. Drain the chick-peas and place in a large saucepan over high heat with water to cover by 2 inches (5 cm). Bring to a boil, reduce the heat to low and simmer gently, uncovered, until the skins begin to split and the beans are tender, 45–60 minutes. Drain and set aside to cool.
3. In a large pot over high heat, bring the 5 qt (5 l) water to a boil. Add the 1 tablespoon salt and the orecchiette and cook according to the package directions or until al dente (see page 10), 12–15 minutes. Drain the orecchiette and toss it immediately with 1 tablespoon of the olive oil. Cover and cool completely in the refrigerator, 1–24 hours.
4. In a large bowl, whisk together the remaining 5 tablespoons (3 fl oz/80 ml) olive oil, vinegar, tomato paste, garlic, cumin and salt and pepper to taste. Add the orecchiette and chopped mint. Toss to mix well.
5. To serve, place in a serving bowl or divide among individual plates and garnish with the mint sprigs. Serve at room temperature.

Serves 6

NUTRITIONAL ANALYSIS: Calories 462 (Kilojoules 1,939); Protein 14 g; Carbohydrates 66 g; Total Fat 17 g; Saturated Fat 2 g; Cholesterol 0 mg; Sodium 246 mg; Dietary Fiber 4 g

FUSILLI, COLORED BEAN AND TOMATO SALAD

Prepare this recipe in summer when vine-ripened cherry tomatoes and fresh green and yellow beans are at their peak of flavor. It pairs well with grilled fish.

5   qt (5 l) water

1   tablespoon salt

12 oz (375 g) dried fusilli

1   tablespoon extra-virgin olive oil

8   oz (250 g) green beans, halved crosswise

8   oz (250 g) yellow beans, halved crosswise

¾ cup (6 fl oz/180 ml) bottled mayonnaise

1   teaspoon Dijon-style mustard

2   teaspoons fresh lemon juice

3   garlic cloves, peeled and minced
    Salt and freshly ground pepper

2   tablespoons warm water

12 red cherry tomatoes, halved

1. In a large pot over high heat, bring the water to a boil. Add the 1 tablespoon salt and the fusilli and cook according to the package directions or until al dente (see page 10), 12–15 minutes. Drain the fusilli and toss it immediately with the olive oil. Cover and cool completely in the refrigerator, 1–24 hours.

2. In a large pot of boiling salted water over high heat, cook the green and yellow beans until tender, 4–6 minutes. Drain and cool completely in the refrigerator.

3. In a small bowl, whisk together the mayonnaise, mustard, lemon juice, garlic and salt and pepper to taste. Whisk in enough of the warm water to thin the mixture and make it barely fluid.

4. In a large bowl, combine the fusilli, mayonnaise mixture, green and yellow beans and tomatoes. Toss to mix well.

5. To serve, place in a serving bowl or divide among individual plates. Serve at room temperature.

Serves 6

NUTRITIONAL ANALYSIS: Calories 458 (Kilojoules 1,924); Protein 9 g; Carbohydrates 52 g; Total Fat 25 g; Saturated Fat 4 g; Cholesterol 16 mg; Sodium 377 mg; Dietary Fiber 4 g

SUMMER VEGETABLE AND FARFALLE SALAD

With bell peppers, carrots, celery and red (Spanish) onion, this salad makes a colorful addition to any barbecue table and goes very well with grilled swordfish.

5 qt (5 l) water
1 tablespoon salt
12 oz (375 g) dried farfalle
6 tablespoons (3 fl oz/90 ml) extra-virgin olive oil
6 tablespoons (3 fl oz/90 ml) red wine vinegar
   Salt and freshly ground pepper
2 carrots, peeled and cut into $\frac{1}{2}$-inch (12-mm) dice
2 celery stalks with leaves, cut into $\frac{1}{2}$-inch (12-mm) dice
1 small red (Spanish) onion, peeled and cut into $\frac{1}{2}$-inch (12-mm) dice
3 small red bell peppers (capsicums), seeded, deribbed and cut into $\frac{1}{2}$-inch (12-mm) dice *(see page 125)*
2 teaspoons finely chopped fresh thyme

1. In a large pot over high heat, bring the water to a boil. Add the 1 tablespoon salt and the farfalle and cook according to the package directions or until al dente (see page 10), 10–12 minutes. Drain the farfalle and toss it immediately with 1 tablespoon of the olive oil. Cover and cool completely in the refrigerator, 1–24 hours.
2. In a large bowl, whisk together the remaining 5 tablespoons (3 fl oz/80 ml) olive oil, vinegar and salt and pepper to taste. Add the farfalle, carrots, celery, onion, peppers and thyme. Toss to mix well.
3. To serve, place in a serving bowl or divide among individual plates. Serve at room temperature.

Serves 6

NUTRITIONAL ANALYSIS: Calories 360 (Kilojoules 1,512); Protein 8 g; Carbohydrates 51 g; Total Fat 15 g; Saturated Fat 2 g; Cholesterol 0 mg; Sodium 216 mg; Dietary Fiber 4 g

RIGATONI AND TOMATO SALAD WITH TAPENADE DRESSING

Black olives, capers, anchovies and garlic lend bite to the dressing for this summertime salad of rigatoni or other medium-sized pasta tubes. If yellow cherry tomatoes are unavailable, use all red ones.

5   qt (5 l) water

1   tablespoon salt

12 oz (375 g) dried rigatoni

3   tablespoons extra-virgin olive oil

⅓   cup (2 oz/60 g) Niçoise or Kalamata olives, pitted

2   tablespoons capers, drained and chopped

2   garlic cloves, peeled and minced

3   anchovy fillets in olive oil, drained and mashed

4   tablespoons (2 fl oz/60 ml) fresh lemon juice

    Salt and freshly ground pepper

12 red cherry tomatoes, halved

12 yellow cherry tomatoes, halved

4   oz (125 g) dried tomatoes in olive oil, drained and cut into ¼-inch (6-mm) strips

    Whole flat-leaf (Italian) parsley leaves

1. In a large pot over high heat, bring the water to a boil. Add the 1 tablespoon salt and the rigatoni and cook according to the package directions or until al dente (see page 10), 12–15 minutes. Drain the rigatoni and toss it immediately with 1 tablespoon of the olive oil. Cover and cool completely in the refrigerator, 1–24 hours.

2. In the work bowl of a food processor with the metal blade or a blender, pulse the olives, capers, garlic and anchovies several times to make a rough paste. Add the lemon juice and the remaining 2 tablespoons olive oil and pulse a few times to make a smoother paste. Add the salt and pepper to taste.

3. In a large bowl, combine the olive mixture, rigatoni, cherry tomatoes and dried tomatoes. Toss to mix well.

4. To serve, place in a serving bowl or divide among individual plates and garnish with the parsley. Serve at room temperature.

Serves 6

NUTRITIONAL ANALYSIS: Calories 391 (Kilojoules 1,640); Protein 9 g; Carbohydrates 52 g; Total Fat 18 g; Saturated Fat 2 g; Cholesterol 1 mg; Sodium 434 mg; Dietary Fiber 4 g

Spring Asparagus and Snap Pea Penne Salad

For a more substantial dish, add fresh fava beans to this bright-tasting salad. Shell them and simmer in a pot of boiling water for 20 seconds. Drain and, when they're cool enough to handle, peel and discard their skins.

5   qt (5 l) water

1   tablespoon salt

12 oz (375 g) dried penne

5   tablespoons (3 fl oz/80 ml) extra-virgin olive oil

8   oz (250 g) asparagus, cut diagonally into 1½-inch (4-cm) pieces

8   oz (250 g) sugar snap peas

1   seedless orange

2   tablespoons red wine vinegar
    Salt and freshly ground pepper

3   tablespoons finely chopped fresh chives

1   orange, cut into 6 wedges

1. In a large pot over high heat, bring the water to a boil. Add the 1 tablespoon salt and the penne and cook according to the package directions or until al dente (see page 10), 10–12 minutes. Drain the penne and toss it immediately with 1 tablespoon of the olive oil. Cover and cool completely in the refrigerator, 1–24 hours.

2. In another large pot of boiling salted water over high heat, cook the asparagus until tender, 4–5 minutes. Using a slotted spoon, remove the asparagus, drain and cool completely in the refrigerator. Add the sugar snap peas to the water, return to a boil and cook until tender, 1–2 minutes. Drain the sugar snap peas and cool completely in the refrigerator.

3. Using a zester or grater, shred the zest of the orange. Then, juice the orange.

4. In a large bowl, whisk together the remaining 4 tablespoons (2 fl oz/60 ml) olive oil, orange zest, orange juice, vinegar and salt and pepper to taste. Add the penne, asparagus, sugar snap peas and chives. Toss to mix well.

5. To serve, place in a serving bowl or divide among individual plates and garnish with the orange wedges. Serve at room temperature.

Serves 6

NUTRITIONAL ANALYSIS: Calories 357 (Kilojoules 1,498); Protein 10 g; Carbohydrates 55 g; Total Fat 13 g; Saturated Fat 2 g; Cholesterol 0 mg; Sodium 364 mg; Dietary Fiber 4 g

ESCAROLE AND ORANGE WITH FUSILLI SALAD

This vivid combination of colors and flavors will brighten even the dreariest of winter days. For variety, try substituting spinach or radicchio for the escarole and walnuts or hazelnuts (filberts) for the pine nuts.

5 qt (5 l) water

1 tablespoon salt

12 oz (375 g) dried fusilli

6 tablespoons (3 fl oz/90 ml) extra-virgin olive oil

4 seedless oranges

1 teaspoon hazelnut (filbert) or walnut oil

3 tablespoons balsamic vinegar

2 garlic cloves, peeled and minced
Salt and freshly ground pepper

1 small head escarole (6 oz/185 g), torn into large bite-sized pieces

⅓ cup (2 oz/60 g) pine nuts, toasted (*see page 124*)

3 tablespoons finely chopped cilantro (fresh coriander)

1. In a large pot over high heat, bring the water to a boil. Add the 1 tablespoon salt and the fusilli and cook according to the package directions or until al dente (see page 10), 10–12 minutes. Drain the fusilli and toss it immediately with 1 tablespoon of the olive oil. Cover and cool completely in the refrigerator, 1–24 hours.

2. Using a knife, peel 3 of the oranges down to the flesh so that no white pith remains. Cut these oranges crosswise into slices ¼-inch (6-mm) thick. Discard the peels.

3. Using a zester or grater, shred the zest of the 1 remaining orange. Then, juice this orange.

4. In a large bowl, whisk together the remaining 5 tablespoons (3 fl oz/80 ml) olive oil, hazelnut or walnut oil, grated orange zest, orange juice, vinegar, garlic and salt and pepper to taste. Add the fusilli, orange slices, escarole, pine nuts and cilantro. Toss to mix well.

5. To serve, place in a serving bowl or divide among individual plates. Serve at room temperature.

Serves 6

NUTRITIONAL ANALYSIS: Calories 440 (Kilojoules 1,846); Protein 10 g; Carbohydrates 59 g; Total Fat 21 g; Saturated Fat 3 g; Cholesterol 0 mg; Sodium 201 mg; Dietary Fiber 6 g

FARFALLE AND FRESH FIG SALAD

Fruit and pasta make an unexpected combination of flavors and textures. Use either red or black figs. In place of the pistachios, you can substitute walnuts, pecans or pine nuts.

5   qt (5 l) water
1   tablespoon salt
12 oz (375 g) dried farfalle
5   tablespoons (3 fl oz/80 ml) extra-virgin olive oil
1   tablespoon hazelnut (filbert) or walnut oil
1   tablespoon sherry vinegar
2   tablespoons white wine vinegar
    Salt and freshly ground pepper
1   lb (500 g) firm ripe figs, halved lengthwise
⅔   cup (3 oz/90 g) shelled unsalted pistachios

1. In a large pot over high heat, bring the water to a boil. Add the 1 tablespoon salt and the farfalle and cook according to the package directions or until al dente (see page 10), 10–12 minutes. Drain the farfalle and toss it immediately with 1 tablespoon of the olive oil. Cover and cool completely in the refrigerator, 1–24 hours.
2. In a large bowl, whisk together the remaining 4 tablespoons (2 fl oz/60 ml) olive oil, hazelnut or walnut oil, sherry vinegar, white wine vinegar and salt and pepper to taste. Add the farfalle, figs and pistachios. Toss to mix well.
3. To serve, place in a serving bowl or divide among individual plates. Serve at room temperature.

Serves 6

NUTRITIONAL ANALYSIS: Calories 473 (Kilojoules 1,986); Protein 10 g; Carbohydrates 63 g; Total Fat 23 g; Saturated Fat 3 g; Cholesterol 0 mg; Sodium 195 mg; Dietary Fiber 4 g

GREENS AND RIGATONI SALAD

A mixture of spinach, arugula, watercress, basil and mint provides vibrant color and refreshing flavor to the dressing for this rigatoni salad. For even more herb flavor, use basil-flavored oil for the dressing.

5 qt (5 l) plus 1 tablespoon water

1 tablespoon salt

12 oz (375 g) dried rigatoni

8 tablespoons (4 fl oz/125 ml) extra-virgin olive oil

2 cups (2 oz/60 g) packed stemmed spinach leaves

1 cup (1 oz/30 g) packed arugula

1 cup (1 oz/30 g) packed stemmed watercress

¼ cup (⅓ oz/10 g) packed fresh basil leaves

3 tablespoons chopped fresh mint leaves

6 tablespoons (3 fl oz/90 ml) fresh lemon juice

Salt and freshly ground pepper

2 small yellow summer squashes, cut into slices ½-inch (12-mm) thick

2 small zucchini (courgettes), cut into slices ½-inch (12-mm) thick

1. Prepare a fire in an outdoor charcoal grill or preheat a broiler (griller).

2. In a large pot over high heat, bring the water to a boil. Add the 1 tablespoon salt and the rigatoni and cook according to the package directions or until al dente (see page 10), 12–15 minutes. Drain the rigatoni and toss it immediately with 1 tablespoon of the olive oil. Cover and cool completely in the refrigerator, 1–24 hours.

3. To make the dressing, in the work bowl of a food processor with the metal blade or a blender, combine 5 tablespoons (3 fl oz/80 ml) of the olive oil and spinach. Process until smooth. Gradually add the arugula, watercress, basil and mint and process until a smooth paste is formed. Add the lemon juice, the 1 tablespoon water and salt and pepper to taste and process until smooth.

4. Coat the squash and zucchini with the remaining 2 tablespoons olive oil. Grill the squash and zucchini over a medium-hot fire or broil (grill), turning occasionally, until golden brown, 3–4 minutes. Set aside to cool.

5. To serve, in a bowl, combine the rigatoni and dressing and top with the squash and zucchini. Divide among individual plates. Serve at room temperature.

Serves 6

NUTRITIONAL ANALYSIS: Calories 392 (Kilojoules 1,645); Protein 8 g; Carbohydrates 49 g; Total Fat 20 g; Saturated Fat 3 g; Cholesterol 0 mg; Sodium 207 mg; Dietary Fiber 3 g

Seafood and Meat Salads

FUSILLI AND SQUID SALAD WITH FENNEL

Light and bright, this seafood salad makes a great main course for six or appetizer for more. If you wish, omit the garlic, and substitute orange juice for the lemon juice.

5   qt (5 l) water

1   tablespoon salt

12 oz (375 g) dried fusilli

6   tablespoons (3 fl oz/90 ml) extra-virgin olive oil

1   lb (500 g) squid

½ cup (4 fl oz/125 ml) Fish Stock *(recipe on page 127)*

5   tablespoons (3 fl oz/80 ml) fresh lemon juice

2   garlic cloves, peeled and minced

1   large fennel bulb, cut into paper-thin lengthwise slices

2   celery stalks, cut diagonally into pieces ½-inch (12-mm) thick

    Salt and freshly ground pepper

¼ cup (½ oz/10 g) finely chopped fresh fennel leaves

1. In a large pot over high heat, bring the water to a boil. Add the 1 tablespoon salt and the fusilli and cook according to the package directions or until al dente (see page 10), 10–12 minutes. Drain the fusilli and toss it immediately with 1 tablespoon of the olive oil. Cover and cool completely in the refrigerator, 1–24 hours.

2. To clean the squid, separate the head from the body by tugging gently. Pull any remaining insides and the transparent quill bone from the body and discard. Remove the tentacles by cutting just below the eyes of the head. Remove and discard the beak by turning the head inside out and pressing the center. Remove and discard the skin from the body by scraping the body with a knife. Cut the body into ½-inch (12-mm) rings, place in a colander, add the tentacles and rinse with water.

3. In a medium frying pan over medium-high heat, bring the Fish Stock to a boil. Add the squid, cover and cook until it turns opaque, about 30 seconds. Using a slotted spoon, remove the squid from the pan and set aside to cool. Boil the cooking liquid, uncovered, over high heat to reduce to 2 tablespoons, 2–3 minutes. Remove from the heat.

4. In a large bowl, whisk together the remaining 5 tablespoons (3 fl oz/80 ml) olive oil, lemon juice and garlic. Add the fusilli, squid, fennel bulb slices, celery and salt and pepper to taste. Toss to mix well.

5. To serve, place in a serving bowl and garnish with the fennel leaves. Serve at room temperature.

Serves 6

NUTRITIONAL ANALYSIS: Calories 401 (Kilojoules 1,685); Protein 17 g; Carbohydrates 49 g; Total Fat 16 g; Saturated Fat 2 g; Cholesterol 138 mg; Sodium 309 mg; Dietary Fiber 3 g

CREAMY SHELL SALAD WITH LOBSTER

Luxurious lobster coated with rose-colored dressing makes this pasta salad an ideal choice for a special luncheon. Fresh crab may replace the lobster, if desired. Serve with white wine.

5 qt (5 l) plus 7 cups (56 fl oz/1.75 l) water

1 tablespoon salt

12 oz (375 g) dried pasta shells

2 tablespoons extra-virgin olive oil

1 live lobster, about 1½ lb (750 g)

½ cup (4 fl oz/125 ml) heavy (double) cream

2 tablespoons tomato paste

3 tablespoons red wine vinegar

   Cayenne pepper

8 red cherry tomatoes, halved

   Salt and freshly ground pepper

   Fresh parsley sprigs

1. In a large pot over high heat, bring the 5 qt (5 l) water to a boil. Add the 1 tablespoon salt and the pasta shells and cook according to the package directions or until al dente (see page 10), 12–15 minutes. Drain the pasta and toss it immediately with 1 tablespoon of the olive oil. Cover and cool completely in the refrigerator, 1–24 hours.

2. In another large pot over high heat, bring the 7 cups (56 fl oz/1.75 l) water to a boil. Add the lobster, immersing completely, and cook until dark red, about 10 minutes. Using tongs, remove the lobster from the pot and set aside to cool. Discard the cooking liquid.

3. When the lobster is cool, crack the claws and remove the meat. Using kitchen shears, cut down the inside of the tail and remove the meat. Dice the meat into ½-inch (12-mm) pieces.

4. In a large bowl, whisk the cream just until it begins to thicken, about 1 minute. Add the remaining 1 tablespoon olive oil, tomato paste, vinegar and cayenne to taste. Whisk until mixed thoroughly. Add the pasta shells, lobster, tomatoes and salt and pepper to taste. Toss to mix well.

5. To serve, place in a serving bowl or divide among individual plates and garnish with the parsley sprigs. Serve at room temperature.

Serves 6

NUTRITIONAL ANALYSIS: Calories 351 (Kilojoules 1,475); Protein 13 g; Carbohydrates 47 g; Total Fat 13 g; Saturated Fat 5 g; Cholesterol 45 mg; Sodium 341 mg; Dietary Fiber 2 g

GRILLED SALMON AND SHELLS SALAD

Caperberries are the edible flower buds of the same plant that produces the more familiar capers, which may be substituted. Soak wooden or bamboo skewers in water to cover for 30 minutes to prevent burning.

5   qt (5 l) water

1   tablespoon salt

10 oz (315 g) dried large pasta shells

7   tablespoons (4 fl oz/100 ml) extra-virgin olive oil

1¼ lb (625 g) salmon fillet, skinned

⅓   cup (3 fl oz/80 ml) fresh lemon juice

1   tablespoon finely chopped fresh oregano

2   teaspoons finely chopped fresh thyme

½   teaspoon finely chopped fresh rosemary

¾   cup (6 oz/185 g) caperberries, drained

    Salt and freshly ground pepper

1. Prepare a fire in an outdoor charcoal grill or preheat a broiler (griller).

2. In a large pot over high heat, bring the water to a boil. Add the 1 tablespoon salt and the pasta shells and cook according to the package directions or until al dente (see page 10), 12–15 minutes. Drain the pasta and toss it immediately with 1 tablespoon of the olive oil. Cover and cool completely in the refrigerator, 1–24 hours.

3. On a cutting surface, cut the salmon into ¾-inch (2-cm) cubes. Thread onto 6 skewers, distributing the cubes evenly. Brush with 1 tablespoon of the olive oil. Grill over a medium-hot fire or broil (grill), turning occasionally, until opaque throughout when pierced with a knife, 5–6 minutes. Set aside until the fish is cool enough to handle. Remove the salmon from the skewers.

4. In a large bowl, whisk together the remaining 5 table-spoons (3 fl oz/80 ml) olive oil, lemon juice, oregano, thyme and rosemary. Add the pasta shells, salmon, caper-berries and salt and pepper to taste. Toss to mix well.

5. To serve, place in a serving bowl or divide among individual plates. Serve at room temperature.

Serves 6

NUTRITIONAL ANALYSIS: Calories 457 (Kilojoules 1,918); Protein 25 g; Carbohydrates 38 g; Total Fat 23 g; Saturated Fat 3 g; Cholesterol 52 mg; Sodium 647 mg; Dietary Fiber 1 g

$\mathcal{S}$HELLS SALAD WITH CLAMS, LEMON AND GARLIC

The sprightly flavor of lemon highlights the fresh clams and garlic in this simple pasta salad. You can also make it with orange juice and garnish with orange wedges.

5 qt (5 l) water

1 tablespoon salt

12 oz (375 g) dried large pasta shells

6 tablespoons (3 fl oz/90 ml) extra-virgin olive oil

4 lb (2 kg) clams, scrubbed well

½ cup (4 fl oz/125 ml) Fish Stock *(recipe on page 127)*

⅓ cup (3 fl oz/80 ml) fresh lemon juice

3 garlic cloves, peeled and minced

½ cup (¾ oz/20 g) finely chopped fresh parsley

Salt and freshly ground pepper

1 lemon, cut into 6 slices

1. In a large pot over high heat, bring the water to a boil. Add the 1 tablespoon salt and the pasta shells and cook according to the package directions or until al dente (see page 10), 12–15 minutes. Drain the pasta and toss it immediately with 1 tablespoon of the olive oil. Cover and cool completely in the refrigerator, 1–24 hours.

2. Discard any clams that do not close to the touch. In a large frying pan, bring the Fish Stock to a boil. Add the clams, reduce the heat to medium, cover and cook, shaking the pan periodically, until the clams open, 3–5 minutes. Using a slotted spoon, lift out the clams and set aside to cool. Discard any unopened clams. Boil the cooking liquid over high heat to reduce it to 2 tablespoons, 3–4 minutes. Remove from the heat.

3. In a large bowl, whisk together the remaining 5 tablespoons (3 fl oz/80 ml) olive oil, lemon juice, garlic and reduced cooking liquid. Add the pasta shells, clams, parsley and salt and pepper to taste. Toss to mix well.

4. To serve, place in a serving bowl or divide among individual plates and garnish with the lemon slices. Serve at room temperature.

Serves 6

NUTRITIONAL ANALYSIS: Calories 374 (Kilojoules 1,571); Protein 13 g; Carbohydrates 49 g; Total Fat 15 g; Saturated Fat 2 g; Cholesterol 15 mg; Sodium 248 mg; Dietary Fiber 2 g

SHELLS, SCALLOPS AND SAFFRON SALAD

You can use either bay or sea scallops in this lively seafood salad; the latter, though, should be cut in halves horizontally before cooking. For the most colorful effect, use a combination of three different bell peppers.

5	qt (5 l) water
1	tablespoon salt
12	oz (375 g) dried large pasta shells
5	tablespoons (3 fl oz/80 ml) extra-virgin olive oil
1	lb (500 g) scallops
1	cup (5 oz/155 g) shelled fresh peas or frozen peas
¼	cup (2 fl oz/60 ml) Champagne vinegar
¼	cup (2 fl oz/60 ml) Fish Stock *(recipe on page 127)*
2	tablespoons tomato paste
1½	teaspoons saffron threads
3	bell peppers (capsicums), roasted, peeled, stemmed, seeded, deribbed and cut into ½-inch (12-mm) strips *(see page 125)*
	Salt and freshly ground pepper

1. In a large pot over high heat, bring the water to a boil. Add the 1 tablespoon salt and the pasta shells and cook according to the package directions or until al dente (see page 10), 12–15 minutes. Drain the pasta and toss it immediately with 1 tablespoon of the olive oil. Cover and cool completely in the refrigerator, 1–24 hours.

2. In a medium frying pan over medium-high heat, warm 1 tablespoon of the olive oil. Add the scallops in batches and sauté, turning once, until opaque throughout about 1 minute on each side. Set aside to cool.

3. In a medium saucepan of boiling salted water over high heat, blanch the peas for 1 minute. Drain immediately and set aside to cool.

4. In a large bowl, whisk together the remaining 3 table-spoons olive oil, vinegar, Fish Stock, tomato paste and saffron. Add the peppers, pasta shells, scallops and salt and pepper to taste. Toss to mix well.

5. To serve, place in a serving bowl or divide among individual plates. Serve at room temperature.

Serves 6

NUTRITIONAL ANALYSIS: Calories 413 (Kilojoules 1,733); Protein 22 g; Carbohydrates 53 g; Total Fat 13 g; Saturated Fat 2 g; Cholesterol 25 mg; Sodium 439 mg; Dietary Fiber 4 g

FUSILLI, SMOKED SALMON AND CAVIAR SALAD

Depending upon the occasion and availability, use domestic sturgeon or salmon roe or, if budget permits, imported beluga, sevruga or osetra caviar. Serve accompanied with Champagne or iced vodka.

5   qt (5 l) water

1   tablespoon salt

12 oz (375 g) dried fusilli

4   tablespoons (2 fl oz/60 ml) extra-virgin olive oil

¼   cup (2 oz/60 g) crème fraîche

5   tablespoons (3 fl oz/80 ml) Champagne vinegar

½   lb (250 g) smoked salmon, cut into thin strips

½   cup (¾ oz/20 g) finely chopped fresh chives

6   green (spring) onions, green and white parts, thinly sliced

     Salt and freshly ground pepper

1   oz (30 g) caviar

8   whole fresh chives

1. In a large pot over high heat, bring the water to a boil. Add the 1 tablespoon salt and the fusilli and cook according to the package directions or until al dente (see page 10), 12–15 minutes. Drain the fusilli and toss it immediately with 1 tablespoon of the olive oil. Cover and cool completely in the refrigerator, 1–24 hours.

2. In a large bowl, whisk together the remaining 3 tablespoons olive oil, crème fraîche and vinegar. Add the fusilli, salmon, chopped chives, green onions and salt and pepper to taste. Toss to mix well.

3. To serve, place in a serving bowl and top with the caviar and whole chives. Serve at room temperature.

Serves 6

NUTRITIONAL ANALYSIS: Calories 374 (Kilojoules 1,571); Protein 16 g; Carbohydrates 46 g; Total Fat 15 g; Saturated Fat 3 g; Cholesterol 41 mg; Sodium 569 mg; Dietary Fiber 2 g

$\mathscr{A}$VOCADO, SHELLS AND SHRIMP SALAD

Avocado halves filled with shrimp are a favorite seafood appetizer. Here, the concept becomes a pasta salad by tossing seafood and shells with a rich purée of avocado and cream. Other seafood may be substituted for the shrimp.

5 qt (5 l) water
1 tablespoon salt
12 oz (375 g) dried pasta shells
3 tablespoons extra-virgin olive oil
½ cup (4 fl oz/125 ml) Fish Stock
   (recipe on page 127)
1 lb (500 g) large shrimp (prawns),
   peeled and deveined *(see page 125)*
1 avocado, halved, peeled and
   seeded
   Cayenne pepper
3 tablespoons white wine vinegar
¼ cup (2 fl oz/60 ml) heavy (double)
   cream
5 green (spring) onions, green and
   white parts, thinly sliced
   Salt and freshly ground pepper

1. In a large pot over high heat, bring the water to a boil. Add the 1 tablespoon salt and the pasta shells and cook according to the package directions or until al dente (see page 10), 12–15 minutes. Drain the pasta and toss it immediately with 1 tablespoon of the olive oil. Cover and cool completely in the refrigerator, 1–24 hours.

2. In a medium frying pan over high heat, bring the Fish Stock to a boil. Add the shrimp, reduce the heat to low, cover and simmer for 1 minute. Stir lightly, re-cover and cook until the shrimp are pink, curled and firm to the touch, about 2 minutes. Using a slotted spoon, remove the shrimp and set aside to cool. Boil the cooking liquid over high heat to reduce it to 2 tablespoons, 1–2 minutes. Remove from the heat.

3. In the work bowl of a food processor with the metal blade or a blender, combine the avocado, cayenne to taste, reduced cooking liquid and vinegar and purée until smooth. With the motor running, add the remaining 2 tablespoons olive oil in a steady stream until it has been completely incorporated. Add the cream and pulse a few times to mix well.

4. In a large bowl, combine the avocado mixture, fusilli, shrimp, green onions and salt and pepper to taste. Toss to mix well.

5. To serve, place in a serving bowl or divide among individual plates. Serve at room temperature.

Serves 6

NUTRITIONAL ANALYSIS: Calories 429 (Kilojoules 1,802); Protein 21 g; Carbohydrates 49 g; Total Fat 18 g; Saturated Fat 4 g; Cholesterol 107 mg; Sodium 320 mg; Dietary Fiber 3 g

MOROCCAN ORECCHIETTE WITH GRILLED FISH SALAD

In Morocco, the simple, robust sauce for this salad is called chermoula, *and tradition holds that, if you gather 30 cooks in one room, you will have 30 different recipes for making it.*

5 qt (5 l) water

1 tablespoon salt

12 oz (375 g) dried orecchiette

5 tablespoons (3 fl oz/80 ml) extra-virgin olive oil

2 teaspoons cumin

1 teaspoon sweet paprika

½ teaspoon ground turmeric

¼ teaspoon cayenne pepper

3 garlic cloves, peeled and minced

½ small yellow onion, peeled and minced

⅓ cup (½ oz/15 g) finely chopped cilantro (fresh coriander)

¼ cup (⅓ oz/10 g) finely chopped fresh parsley

⅓ cup (3 fl oz/80 ml) fresh lemon juice
Salt and freshly ground pepper

1 lb (500 g) fresh tuna or swordfish fillet

1 lemon, cut into 6 wedges

1. Prepare a fire in an outdoor charcoal grill or preheat a broiler (griller).

2. In a large pot over high heat, bring the water to a boil. Add the 1 tablespoon salt and the orecchiette and cook according to the package directions or until al dente (see page 10), 12–15 minutes. Drain the orecchiette and toss it immediately with 1 tablespoon of the olive oil. Cover and cool completely in the refrigerator, 1–24 hours.

3. To make the sauce, in the work bowl of a food processor with the metal blade or a blender, combine the cumin, paprika, turmeric, cayenne, garlic, onion, cilantro, parsley, lemon juice, 3 tablespoons of the olive oil and salt and pepper to taste and purée until smooth.

4. Coat the tuna or swordfish with the remaining 1 table-spoon olive oil. Grill the fish over a medium-hot fire or broil (grill), turning occasionally, until opaque throughout when pierced with a knife, 6–8 minutes. Set aside until the fish is cool enough to handle. Place on a cutting surface and cut into 1-inch (2.5-cm) cubes.

5. In a large bowl, combine the sauce, orecchiette and fish. Toss to mix well.

6. To serve, place in a serving bowl or divide among individual plates and garnish with the lemon wedges. Serve at room temperature.

Serves 6

NUTRITIONAL ANALYSIS: Calories 436 (Kilojoules 1,832); Protein 25 g; Carbohydrates 49 g; Total Fat 17 g; Saturated Fat 3 g; Cholesterol 29 mg; Sodium 227 mg; Dietary Fiber 2 g

SCALLOP AND CHEESE TORTELLINI SALAD

Slightly sweet in flavor, scallops seem to have a natural affinity with cheese, making them an ideal choice for pairing with tortellini. Use either bay or larger sea scallops, cutting the latter in half horizontally.

5   qt (5 l) water

1   tablespoon salt

12 oz (375 g) cheese tortellini

5   tablespoons (3 fl oz/80 ml) extra-virgin olive oil

1   lb (500 g) scallops

3   tablespoons red wine vinegar

½   cup (3½ oz/105 g) green olives, pitted and coarsely chopped

½   cup (3½ oz/105 g) black olives, pitted and coarsely chopped

2   tablespoons finely chopped fresh parsley

Salt and freshly ground pepper

1. In a large pot over high heat, bring the water to a boil. Add the 1 tablespoon salt and the tortellini and cook according to the package directions or until al dente (see page 10), 10–12 minutes for dried, 4–5 minutes for fresh. Drain the tortellini and toss them immediately with 1 tablespoon of the olive oil. Cover and cool completely in the refrigerator, 1–24 hours.

2. In a medium frying pan over medium-high heat, heat 1 tablespoon of the olive oil. Add the scallops and sauté, turning once, until opaque throughout when pierced with a knife, about 1 minute on each side. Set aside to cool.

3. In a large bowl, whisk together the remaining 3 tablespoons olive oil and vinegar. Add the tortellini, scallops, green and black olives, parsley and salt and pepper to taste. Toss to mix well.

4. To serve, place in a serving bowl or divide among individual plates. Serve at room temperature.

Serves 6

NUTRITIONAL ANALYSIS: Calories 374 (Kilojoules 1,570); Protein 20 g; Carbohydrates 31 g; Total Fat 19 g; Saturated Fat 4 g; Cholesterol 48 mg; Sodium 926 mg; Dietary Fiber 1 g

RIGATONI AND MUSSELS SALAD

The flavors of mussels, thyme and cream marry well in this pasta salad inspired by foods popular in the south of France. Provide extra bowls for the shells; guests will be shelling the mussels at the table.

5 qt (5 l) water

1 tablespoon salt

12 oz (375 g) dried rigatoni

4 tablespoons (2 fl oz/60 ml) extra-virgin olive oil

½ cup (4 fl oz/125 ml) Fish Stock *(recipe on page 127)*

12 fresh thyme sprigs

6 shallots, peeled and minced

2 lb (1 kg) mussels, debearded and scrubbed well

¼ cup (2 fl oz/60 ml) heavy (double) cream

¼ cup (2 fl oz/60 ml) fresh lemon juice

2 teaspoons finely chopped fresh thyme

Salt and freshly ground pepper

1 lemon, cut into 6 wedges

1. In a large pot over high heat, bring the water to a boil. Add the 1 tablespoon salt and the rigatoni and cook according to the package directions or until al dente (see page 10), 12–15 minutes. Drain the rigatoni and toss it immediately with 1 tablespoon of the olive oil. Cover and cool completely in the refrigerator, 1–24 hours.

2. In a large frying pan over high heat, bring the Fish Stock, 6 of the thyme sprigs and shallots to a boil. Discard any mussels that do not close to the touch. Add the mussels, reduce the heat to medium, cover and cook, shaking the pan periodically, until the mussels open, 2–4 minutes. Using a slotted spoon, lift out the mussels and set aside to cool. Discard any unopened mussels. Boil the cooking liquid over high heat to reduce it to 2 tablespoons, 3–4 minutes. Remove from the heat. Remove and discard the thyme sprigs.

3. In a large bowl, whisk together the remaining 3 tablespoons olive oil, cream, lemon juice, reduced cooking liquid, chopped thyme and salt and pepper to taste. Add the rigatoni and mussels. Toss to mix well.

4. To serve, place in a serving bowl or divide among individual plates and garnish with the remaining thyme sprigs and lemon wedges. Serve at room temperature.

Serves 6

NUTRITIONAL ANALYSIS: Calories 375 (Kilojoules 1,577); Protein 13 g; Carbohydrates 50 g; Total Fat 15 g; Saturated Fat 4 g; Cholesterol 26 mg; Sodium 351 mg; Dietary Fiber 2 g

SALSA VERDE SHELLS AND SHRIMP SALAD

The Italian "green sauce" that dresses this pasta salad gets its bright color and rich aroma from a mixture of fresh herbs, capers, garlic and lemon juice. If you like, substitute bay or sea scallops, clams or mussels for the shrimp.

5 qt (5 l) water

1 tablespoon salt

12 oz (375 g) dried large pasta shells

6 tablespoons (3 fl oz/90 ml) extra-virgin olive oil

½ cup (4 fl oz/125 ml) Fish Stock *(recipe on page 127)*

1 lb (500 g) large shrimp (prawns), shelled and deveined *(see page 125)*

¾ cup (1 oz/30 g) finely chopped fresh parsley

⅓ cup (½ oz/15 g) finely chopped fresh chives

¾ teaspoon finely chopped fresh thyme

¾ teaspoon finely chopped fresh oregano

¼ cup (2 oz/60 g) capers, drained and chopped

3 garlic cloves, peeled and minced

6 tablespoons (3 fl oz/90 ml) fresh lemon juice

Salt and freshly ground pepper

1 lemon, cut into 6 slices

1. In a large pot over high heat, bring the water to a boil. Add the 1 tablespoon salt and the pasta shells and cook according to the package directions or until al dente (see page 10), 12–15 minutes. Drain the pasta and toss it immediately with 1 tablespoon of the olive oil. Cover and cool completely in the refrigerator, 1–24 hours.

2. In a large frying pan over high heat, bring the Fish Stock to a boil. Add the shrimp, reduce the heat to low, cover and simmer for 1 minute. Stir lightly, re-cover and cook until the shrimp are pink, curled and firm to the touch, about 2 minutes. Using a slotted spoon, remove the shrimp from the pan and set aside to cool. Boil the cooking liquid over high heat to reduce it to 2 tablespoons, about 2 minutes. Remove from the heat.

3. In a large bowl, whisk together the remaining 5 table-spoons (3 fl oz/80 ml) olive oil, parsley, chives, thyme, oregano, capers, garlic, lemon juice and reduced cooking liquid. Add the pasta shells, shrimp and salt and pepper to taste. Toss to mix well.

4. To serve, place in a serving bowl or divide among individual plates and garnish with the lemon slices. Serve at room temperature.

Serves 6

NUTRITIONAL ANALYSIS: Calories 407 (Kilojoules 1,710); Protein 20 g; Carbohydrates 48 g; Total Fat 16 g; Saturated Fat 2 g; Cholesterol 93 mg; Sodium 460 mg; Dietary Fiber 2 g

HERBED FARFALLE AND BEEF SALAD

The combination of fresh herbs and lemon juice makes this salad featuring beef steak particularly refreshing. Other medium-sized pasta shapes may be used in place of the farfalle.

5 qt (5 l) water

1 tablespoon salt

12 oz (375 g) dried farfalle

7 tablespoons (4 fl oz/100 ml) extra-virgin olive oil

12 oz (375 g) New York strip, top round or filet mignon beef steak

   Salt and freshly ground pepper

5 tablespoons (3 fl oz/80 ml) fresh lemon juice

3 garlic cloves, peeled and minced

1 teaspoon ground cumin

¼ cup (⅓ oz/10 g) packed fresh flat-leaf (Italian) parsley leaves

1 cup (1 oz/30 g) packed cilantro (fresh coriander) sprigs

½ cup (½ oz/15 g) packed fresh basil leaves, torn

¼ cup (⅓ oz/10 g) packed fresh mint leaves

1 cup (1 oz/30 g) packed arugula

1. In a large pot over high heat, bring the water to a boil. Add the 1 tablespoon salt and the farfalle and cook according to the package directions or until al dente (see page 10), 10–12 minutes. Drain the farfalle and toss it immediately with 1 tablespoon of the olive oil. Cover and cool completely in the refrigerator, 1–24 hours.

2. In a medium frying pan over medium heat, heat 1 tablespoon of the olive oil. Add the steak and cook until golden on one side, 4 minutes. Turn over the steak, add salt and pepper to taste and continue to cook to the desired doneness or until there is resistance to the touch, 5–6 minutes longer. Place on a work surface and cut into slices.

3. In a large bowl, whisk together the remaining 5 tablespoons (3 fl oz/80 ml) olive oil, lemon juice, garlic and cumin. Add the farfalle, steak, parsley, cilantro, basil, mint and arugula. Toss to mix well.

4. To serve, place in a serving bowl or divide among individual plates. Serve at room temperature.

Serves 6

NUTRITIONAL ANALYSIS: Calories 465 (Kilojoules 1,952); Protein 20 g; Carbohydrates 47 g; Total Fat 23 g; Saturated Fat 4 g; Cholesterol 35 mg; Sodium 228 mg; Dietary Fiber 2 g

GREEN PEAS AND PASTA SALAD

Rich, colorful and with a distinctive edge of smoky sweetness, this salad is a traditional picnic favorite. Smoked turkey or chicken may replace the ham. Blanch a few whole pea pods as garnish, if desired.

5 qt (5 l) water

1 tablespoon salt

12 oz (375 g) dried large elbow pasta

4 tablespoons (2 fl oz/60 ml) extra-virgin olive oil

1 cup (5 oz/155 g) fresh shelled peas or frozen peas

¼ cup (2 fl oz/60 ml) heavy (double) cream

3 tablespoons red wine vinegar

½ cup (2 oz/60 g) finely grated Parmesan cheese

6 oz (185 g) smoked ham (Virginia, Smithfield, Black Forest or Westphalian), cut into thin strips

Salt and freshly ground pepper

Fresh parsley sprigs

1. In a large pot over high heat, bring the water to a boil. Add the 1 tablespoon salt and the elbow pasta and cook according to the package directions or until al dente (see page 10), 7–10 minutes. Drain the pasta and toss it immediately with 1 tablespoon of the olive oil. Cover and cool completely in the refrigerator, 1–24 hours.

2. In a medium saucepan of boiling salted water over high heat, blanch the peas for 1 minute. Drain immediately and set aside to cool.

3. In a large bowl, whisk together the remaining 3 tablespoons olive oil, cream, vinegar and Parmesan cheese. Add the elbow pasta, peas, ham and salt and pepper to taste. Toss to mix well.

4. To serve, place in a serving bowl or divide among individual plates and garnish with the parsley sprigs. Serve at room temperature.

Serves 6

NUTRITIONAL ANALYSIS: Calories 419 (Kilojoules 1,759); Protein 17 g; Carbohydrates 49 g; Total Fat 18 g; Saturated Fat 6 g; Cholesterol 33 mg; Sodium 820 mg; Dietary Fiber 3 g

FUSILLI AND LAMB SALAD WITH MINT DRESSING

The lamb and the eggplant (aubergine) may be grilled and combined with the pasta up to 8 hours ahead. Add the mint dressing at the last minute so it stays bright green.

5	qt (5 l) water
1	tablespoon salt
12	oz (375 g) dried fusilli
7	tablespoons (4 fl oz/100 ml) extra-virgin olive oil
3	slender (Asian) eggplants (aubergines), halved lengthwise
1½	lb (750 g) boneless leg of lamb, butterflied and trimmed of fat
3	tablespoons red wine vinegar
2	garlic cloves, peeled and minced
¼	cup (⅓ oz/10 g) finely chopped fresh mint
4	plum (Roma) tomatoes, sliced
	Salt and freshly ground pepper
	Fresh mint sprigs

1. Prepare a fire in an outdoor charcoal grill or preheat a broiler (griller).

2. In a large pot over high heat, bring the water to a boil. Add the 1 tablespoon salt and the fusilli and cook according to the package directions or until al dente (see page 10), 10–12 minutes. Drain the fusilli and toss it immediately with 1 tablespoon of the olive oil. Cover and cool completely in the refrigerator, 1–24 hours.

3. Brush the lamb with 1 tablespoon of the olive oil. Grill the lamb over a medium-hot fire or broil (grill), turning once, 8–10 minutes on each side. Test by cutting a small slit in the thickest part. The meat should be slightly pink on the inside and well browned on the outside. Place on a work surface and cut the meat across the grain into thin strips.

4. Brush the eggplant with 2 tablespoons of the olive oil. Grill or broil, turning once, until golden, 3–5 minutes on each side. Cool and cut into slices.

5. In a large bowl, whisk together the remaining 3 tablespoons olive oil, vinegar, garlic and chopped mint. Add the fusilli, lamb, eggplant, tomatoes and salt and pepper to taste. Toss to mix well.

6. To serve, place in a serving bowl or divide among individual plates and garnish with the mint sprigs. Serve at room temperature.

Serves 6

NUTRITIONAL ANALYSIS: Calories 518 (Kilojoules 2,176); Protein 31 g; Carbohydrates 49 g; Total Fat 23 g; Saturated Fat 4 g; Cholesterol 73 mg; Sodium 269 mg; Dietary Fiber 3 g

 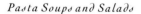

WARM LINGUINE SALAD WITH BACON AND GOAT CHEESE

If you like, the bacon may be omitted for a vegetarian version of this main course salad. Breaking the linguine pieces before cooking makes it easier to eat, but they can be left long for a more dramatic presentation.

5 qt (5 l) water

1 tablespoon salt

12 oz (375 g) dried linguine, broken into 3-inch (7.5-cm) pieces

6 tablespoons (3 fl oz/90 ml) extra-virgin olive oil

3 oz (90 g) bacon, cut into 1-inch (2.5-cm) squares

2 garlic cloves, peeled and minced

3 tablespoons balsamic vinegar

2 cups (2 oz/60 g) packed arugula
Salt and freshly ground pepper

1 cup (4 oz/125 g) fine dried bread crumbs

12 oz (375 g) fresh goat cheese, cut into 6 pieces

1. Preheat an oven to 400°F (200°C).

2. In a large pot over high heat, bring the water to a boil. Add the 1 tablespoon salt and the linguine and cook according to the package directions or until al dente (see page 10), 5–8 minutes. Drain the linguine and toss it immediately with 1 tablespoon of the olive oil.

3. In a large frying pan over medium heat, fry the bacon, uncovered, stirring occasionally, until golden and crisp, about 5 minutes. Reduce the heat to low, add the garlic and continue to cook uncovered for 1 minute. Add 3 tablespoons of the olive oil, vinegar, linguine, arugula and salt and pepper to taste. Warm over low heat until the pasta is heated through, about 1 minute.

4. Place the bread crumbs in a shallow bowl. Coat the goat cheese pieces with the remaining 2 tablespoons olive oil and then roll them in the bread crumbs. Place on a baking sheet. Bake until warm and slightly bubbling around the edges, about 4 minutes.

5. To serve, place the warm pasta mixture in a serving bowl or divide among individual plates and top with the goat cheese.

Serves 6

NUTRITIONAL ANALYSIS: Calories 640 (Kilojoules 2,686); Protein 21 g; Carbohydrates 59 g; Total Fat 36 g; Saturated Fat 14 g; Cholesterol 36 mg; Sodium 667 mg; Dietary Fiber 3 g

PROSCIUTTO AND PENNE SQUASH SALAD

This colorful salad presents a rich array of satisfying tastes and textures. Other varieties of squash may be substituted for the butternut and crisply cooked bacon may replace the prosciutto.

5 qt (5 l) water

1 tablespoon salt

12 oz (375 g) dried penne

7 tablespoons (4 fl oz/100 ml) extra-virgin olive oil

1½ lb (750 g) butternut squash, peeled, seeded and cut into ½-inch (12-mm) cubes

⅓ cup (3 fl oz/80 ml) fresh orange juice

3 tablespoons balsamic vinegar

2 tablespoons red wine vinegar

1 teaspoon grated orange zest

¼ teaspoon freshly grated nutmeg

4 oz (125 g) thinly sliced prosciutto, cut into thin strips

¼ cup (1 oz/30 g) grated Parmesan cheese

Salt and freshly ground pepper

1. Preheat an oven to 400°F (200°C).

2. In a large pot over high heat, bring the water to a boil. Add the 1 tablespoon salt and the penne and cook according to the package directions or until al dente (see page 10), 10–12 minutes. Drain the penne and toss it immediately with 1 tablespoon of the olive oil. Cover and cool completely in the refrigerator, 1–24 hours.

3. Coat the squash cubes with 2 tablespoons of the olive oil. Spread them in a single layer on a baking sheet. Bake, turning occasionally, until golden, about 20 minutes. Set aside to cool.

4. In a large bowl, whisk together the remaining 4 tablespoons (2 fl oz/60 ml) olive oil, orange juice, balsamic vinegar, red wine vinegar, orange zest and nutmeg. Add the penne, squash, prosciutto, Parmesan cheese and salt and pepper to taste. Toss to mix well.

5. To serve, place in a serving bowl or divide among individual plates. Serve at room temperature.

Serves 6

NUTRITIONAL ANALYSIS: Calories 463 (Kilojoules 1,946); Protein 15 g; Carbohydrates 57 g; Total Fat 21 g; Saturated Fat 4 g; Cholesterol 19 mg; Sodium 623 mg; Dietary Fiber 4 g

ORECCHIETTE AND SALAMI SALAD

Zesty, cool and colorful, this pasta salad is an ideal main course for a hot summer evening. Try other medium-sized pasta shapes instead of the orecchiette, if you like.

5 qt (5 l) water

1 tablespoon salt

12 oz (375 g) dried orecchiette

6 tablespoons (3 fl oz/90 ml) extra-virgin olive oil

1 cup (6 oz/185 g) fresh or frozen corn kernels (about 2 ears of corn)

3 tablespoons red wine vinegar

2 garlic cloves, peeled and minced

3 anchovy fillets in olive oil, drained and mashed

3 tablespoons capers, drained

5 oz (155 g) salami, thinly sliced and cut into thin strips

1 *each* red, yellow and green bell pepper (capsicum), seeded, deribbed and diced *(see page 125)*

1 small red (Spanish) onion, peeled and diced

Salt and freshly ground pepper

1. In a large pot over high heat, bring the water to a boil. Add the 1 tablespoon salt and the orecchiette and cook according to the package directions or until al dente (see page 10), 12–15 minutes. Drain the orecchiette and toss it immediately with 1 tablespoon of the olive oil. Cover and cool completely in the refrigerator, 1–24 hours.

2. In a medium saucepan of boiling salted water over high heat, blanch the corn for 1 minute. Drain immediately and set aside to cool.

3. In a large bowl, whisk together the remaining 5 tablespoons (3 fl oz/80 ml) olive oil, vinegar, garlic, anchovies and capers. Add the orecchiette, corn, salami, peppers, red onion and salt and pepper to taste. Toss to mix well.

4. To serve, place in a serving bowl or divide among individual plates. Serve at room temperature.

Serves 6

NUTRITIONAL ANALYSIS: Calories 475 (Kilojoules 1,994); Protein 14 g; Carbohydrates 54 g; Total Fat 24 g; Saturated Fat 5 g; Cholesterol 20 mg; Sodium 888 mg; Dietary Fiber 4 g

FUSILLI AND MORTADELLA SALAD

Use other medium-sized pasta shapes in place of the fusilli and substitute such cured meats as salami, prosciutto, coppacola or smoked turkey or chicken for the mortadella, if desired.

5   qt (5 l) water

1   tablespoon salt

12 oz (375 g) dried fusilli

4   tablespoons (2 fl oz/60 ml) extra-virgin olive oil

¼ cup (2 fl oz/60 ml) heavy (double) cream

¼ cup (2 fl oz/60 ml) fresh lemon juice

3   garlic cloves, peeled and minced

6   oz (185 g) thinly sliced mortadella, cut into thin strips

1   cup (1 oz/30 g) packed fresh flat-leaf (Italian) parsley leaves

½ cup (2 oz/60 g) grated Parmesan cheese
    Salt and freshly ground pepper

1. In a large pot over high heat, bring the water to a boil. Add the 1 tablespoon salt and the fusilli and cook according to the package directions or until al dente (see page 10), 10–12 minutes. Drain the fusilli and toss it immediately with 1 tablespoon of the olive oil. Cover and cool completely in the refrigerator, 1–24 hours.

2. In a large bowl, whisk together the remaining 3 tablespoons olive oil, cream, lemon juice and garlic. Add the fusilli, mortadella, parsley, Parmesan cheese and salt and pepper to taste. Toss to mix well.

3. To serve, place in a serving dish or divide among individual plates. Serve at room temperature.

Serves 6

NUTRITIONAL ANALYSIS: Calories 456 (Kilojoules 1,914); Protein 15 g; Carbohydrates 47 g; Total Fat 24 g; Saturated Fat 8 g; Cholesterol 36 mg; Sodium 704 mg; Dietary Fiber 2 g

SPICY PENNE AND HOT PEPPER CHICKEN SALAD

In Italy, one version of this salad is known as pollo forte, *strong chicken —
a reference to the powerful, pleasing aroma and taste resulting from its
combination of balsamic vinegar, garlic, red onion and hot chili pepper.*

5   qt (5 l) water

1   tablespoon salt

12 oz (375 g) dried penne

7   tablespoons (4 fl oz/100 ml) extra-
    virgin olive oil

1   lb (500 g) skinned and boned
    chicken breast meat (about 1 large
    whole breast)
    Salt and freshly ground pepper

3   tablespoons red wine vinegar

3   tablespoons balsamic vinegar

2   garlic cloves, peeled and minced

½   *each* red, yellow and green bell
    pepper (capsicum), seeded,
    deribbed and thinly sliced
    (see page 125)

1   large jalapeño pepper, seeded and
    minced

½   small red (Spanish) onion, peeled
    and thinly sliced

24 fresh large basil leaves

12 red cherry tomatoes

1. In a large pot over high heat, bring the water to a boil.
Add the 1 tablespoon salt and the penne and cook according to the package directions or until al dente (see page 10),
10–12 minutes. Drain the penne and toss it immediately
with 1 tablespoon of the olive oil. Cover and cool completely
in the refrigerator, 1–24 hours.

2. In a medium frying pan over medium heat, heat 1 tablespoon of the olive oil. Add the chicken and cook until
golden on one side, about 4 minutes. Turn over the chicken,
season with salt and pepper to taste and continue to cook
until opaque throughout when pierced with a knife, 6–8
minutes longer. Place on a cutting surface and cut the
chicken on the diagonal into thin strips. Set aside to cool.

3. In a large bowl, whisk together the remaining 5 tablespoons (3 fl oz/80 ml) olive oil, red wine vinegar, balsamic
vinegar and garlic. Add the penne, chicken, peppers,
jalapeño and red onion. Toss to mix well.

4. To serve, place in a serving bowl or divide among
individual plates and garnish with the basil leaves and
cherry tomatoes. Serve at room temperature.

Serves 6

NUTRITIONAL ANALYSIS: Calories 455 (Kilojoules 1,913); Protein 25 g; Carbohydrates 49 g;
Total Fat 18 g; Saturated Fat 3 g; Cholesterol 44 mg; Sodium 247 mg; Dietary Fiber 3 g

CHICKEN AND MUSHROOM FUSILLI SALAD WITH HERBS

Fresh herbs enliven the simple dressing for this springtime salad. Use other medium-sized pasta shapes instead of the fusilli, if you like. For added flavor, use an herb-flavored oil rather than plain olive oil in the dressing.

5   qt (5 l) water

1   tablespoon salt

12   oz (375 g) dried fusilli

7   tablespoons (4 fl oz/100 ml) extra-virgin olive oil

1   large whole chicken breast, skinned and boned (about 1 lb/500 g meat)   Salt and freshly ground pepper

1   cup (8 fl oz/250 ml) Chicken Stock *(recipe on page 127)*

3   tablespoons red wine vinegar

1½   tablespoons balsamic vinegar

1   tablespoon finely chopped fresh sage

1½   teaspoons finely chopped fresh thyme

½   teaspoon finely chopped fresh rosemary

8   oz (250 g) fresh mushrooms, thinly sliced

1. In a large pot over high heat, bring the water to a boil. Add the 1 tablespoon salt and the fusilli and cook according to the package directions or until al dente (see page 10), 10–12 minutes. Drain the fusilli and toss it immediately with 1 tablespoon of the olive oil. Cover and cool completely in the refrigerator, 1–24 hours.

2. In a medium frying pan over medium heat, warm 1 tablespoon of the olive oil. Add the chicken and cook until golden on one side, about 4 minutes. Turn over the chicken, add salt and pepper to taste and continue to cook until opaque throughout when pierced with a knife, 6–8 minutes longer. Add the Chicken Stock and stir over high heat, scraping the bottom of the pan to loosen the cooked bits, and boil to reduce the liquid to about ¼ cup (2 fl oz/60 ml), about 5 minutes. Using a slotted spoon, remove the chicken, reserving the cooking liquid. Place the chicken on a work surface and cut on the diagonal into thin strips. Set aside to cool.

3. In a large bowl, whisk together the remaining 5 tablespoons (3 fl oz/80 ml) olive oil, red wine vinegar, balsamic vinegar, sage, thyme, rosemary and ¼ cup (2 fl oz/60 ml) of the reduced cooking liquid. Add the fusilli and mushrooms. Toss to mix well.

4. To serve, place in a serving bowl or divide among individual plates and top with the chicken strips. Serve at room temperature.

Serves 6

NUTRITIONAL ANALYSIS: Calories 450 (Kilojoules 1,889); Protein 26 g; Carbohydrates 47 g; Total Fat 19 g; Saturated Fat 3 g; Cholesterol 44 mg; Sodium 264 mg; Dietary Fiber 2 g

GARLIC LOVER'S PENNE AND CHICKEN SALAD

If you're a devotee of garlic, this salad is a real treat. Cooked for almost 30 minutes, the garlic here loses its strong, assertive flavor and develops a sweet, nutty taste that perfectly complements the chicken and pasta.

5	qt (5 l) water
1	tablespoon salt
12	oz (375 g) dried penne
7	tablespoons (4 fl oz/100 ml) extra-virgin olive oil
1	lb (500 g) skinned and boned chicken breast meat (about 1 large whole breast)
	Salt and freshly ground pepper
24	garlic cloves, peeled
2½	cups (20 fl oz/625 ml) Chicken Stock *(recipe on page 127)*
3	tablespoons red wine vinegar
2	teaspoons finely chopped fresh rosemary
2	tablespoons finely chopped fresh parsley
	Fresh rosemary sprigs

1. In a large pot over high heat, bring the water to a boil. Add the 1 tablespoon salt and the penne and cook according to the package directions or until al dente (see page 10), 10–12 minutes. Drain the penne and toss it immediately with 1 tablespoon of the olive oil. Cover and cool completely in the refrigerator, 1–24 hours.

2. In a medium frying pan over medium heat, warm 1 tablespoon of the olive oil. Add the chicken and cook until golden on one side, about 4 minutes. Turn over the chicken, season with salt and pepper to taste and continue to cook until opaque throughout when pierced with a knife, 6–8 minutes longer. Using a spatula, remove the chicken, reserving the frying pan. Place the chicken on a work surface and cut on the diagonal into thin strips. Let cool.

3. To the reserved frying pan over medium heat, add the garlic and cook, uncovered, stirring occasionally, until golden brown, 3–4 minutes. Add the Chicken Stock and continue to cook until the stock has reduced to 2 tablespoons and the garlic is soft, 20–25 minutes. Using a slotted spoon, remove the garlic from the pan and cool, reserving the reduced cooking liquid.

4. In a large bowl, whisk together the remaining 5 tablespoons (3 fl oz/80 ml) olive oil, reduced cooking liquid, vinegar, chopped rosemary and parsley. Add the penne, chicken and garlic cloves. Toss to mix well.

5. To serve, place in a serving bowl and garnish with the rosemary sprigs. Serve at room temperature.

Serves 6

NUTRITIONAL ANALYSIS: Calories 464 (Kilojoules 1,950); Protein 27 g; Carbohydrates 49 g; Total Fat 19 g; Saturated Fat 3 g; Cholesterol 44 mg; Sodium 294 mg; Dietary Fiber 2 g

Basic Terms and Techniques

This glossary provides a reference source for this volume, with descriptions of ingredients, definitions of terms and explanations of fundamental food preparation and cooking techniques.

BEANS AND LENTILS

All manner of dried beans and lentils may be combined with pasta to make hearty soups or salads. When eaten in combination with pasta, beans and lentils make a complete protein; this is especially important for anyone eating a vegetarian diet.

To Prepare Beans and Lentils: Before use, dried beans and lentils should be carefully picked over to remove any that are discolored or misshapen, or any impurities such as small stones or fibers. Soak beans in cold water to cover to shorten their cooking time and improve their digestibility, from 3 hours to overnight. Lentils require no presoaking.

BLANCH

To partially cook food by immersing it in a large quantity of boiling water for anywhere from a few seconds to a few minutes, depending upon the food, its size and how it will be used in a recipe.

CHEESES

Many different types of cheese complement the taste and texture of pasta.

To Grate and Shave Cheese: In most cases, firm- to hard-textured cheeses should be grated with the fine rasps of a cheese grater. Cut softer cheeses into thin pieces with the small holes of a shredder; the finer the particles of cheese, the more readily they will melt into a soup or mix with other salad ingredients. Thin shavings of cheese, cut with a cheese shaver or a swivel-bladed vegetable peeler, make an attractive and flavorful garnish for both soups and salads.

GRUYÈRE A variety of Swiss cheese, Gruyère has a firm, smooth texture, small holes and a strong, nutty flavor.

GORGONZOLA A creamy, blue-veined Italian cheese. Other creamy blue cheeses may be substituted.

MOZZARELLA A rindless white, mild-tasting Italian cheese traditionally made from water buffalo's milk and sold fresh. Commercially produced and packaged cow's-milk mozzarella has less flavor. Look for fresh mozzarella, which is sold immersed in water. Mozzarella may be smoked, yielding a firmer textured, aromatic but still mild cheese.

PARMESAN A semi-hard cheese made from half skim and half whole cow's milk, with a sharp, salty flavor that results from up to two years of aging. In its prime, a good piece of Parmesan cheese is dry but not grainy and flakes easily. For best flavor, buy in block form and grate just before use.

EMULSIFY

To combine two liquids that would not ordinarily blend, such as vinegar and oil, by causing tiny droplets of one to be suspended in another. In a vinaigrette dressing, for example, an emulsion is made by whisking the vinegar briskly or processing in a food processor or blender while oil is added in a thin, steady stream.

GARLIC

Popular worldwide as a flavoring ingredient, either raw or cooked, this pungent bulb is best purchased in whole heads so that the cloves can be separated from the head as needed. Don't purchase more than you will use within 1–2 weeks, as garlic can lose its flavor with prolonged storage.

HERBS

A wide variety of fresh and dried herbs add flavor, aroma and color to pasta soups and salads. Keep fresh herbs in water—as you would cut flowers—awaiting use. They will last up to 1 week if trimmed daily and refrigerated. Store dried herbs in tightly covered containers in a cool dark place and use within 6 months of purchase.

NUTS

Many varieties of nuts may be used to add a rich flavor and crunchy texture to pasta salads.

ALMONDS Mellow, sweet-flavored nuts, an important crop in California and popular throughout the world.

PINE NUTS Small, ivory seeds extracted from the cones of a species of pine tree, with a rich, slightly resinous flavor. Widely used in Southwestern and Middle Eastern cuisines.

PISTACHIOS Slightly sweet, full-flavored nuts with a distinctively green, crunchy meat. Native to Asia Minor,

To Peel and Mince a Garlic Clove

1. To peel, place the clove on a work surface and cover it with the side of a large knife. Press down to crush the clove slightly; slip off the dry skin.

2. To mince, use a sharp knife to cut the peeled clove into thin slices. Then cut across the slices to make thin strips.

3. Using a gentle rocking motion, cut back and forth across the strips to mince them into fine particles.

4. Alternatively, press the peeled clove through a garlic press.

they are grown primarily in the Middle East and California.

WALNUTS Rich, crisp-textured nuts with distinctively crinkled surfaces. English walnuts, the most familiar variety, are grown worldwide, although the largest crops are in California.

To Toast Nuts: Toasting brings out the full flavor and aroma of nuts. To toast any kind of nut, preheat an oven to 325°F (165°C). Spread the nuts in a single layer on a baking sheet and toast in the oven until they just begin to change color, 5–10 minutes. Cool to room temperature. Alternatively, toast nuts in a dry, heavy frying pan over low heat, stirring frequently to prevent scorching, 3–5 minutes.

OLIVE OIL

Olive oil plays several important roles in the preparation of pasta soups and salads. Olive oil is often used to sauté ingredients, and to impart both flavor and a smooth texture to dressings. Olive oil is stirred into cooked pasta for salad to keep it from sticking together; a small amount of flavorful oil may be used as a seasoning for a soup, drizzled into individual bowls at the last minute to release its perfume. For the best flavor, use extra-virgin olive oil for dressing. Pure olive oil can be used for cooking.

Store all oils in tightly covered containers in a cool, dark place.

OLIVES

A specialty of the cuisines of Mediterranean Europe, and popularized by them around the world, ripe black olives—cured in combinations of salt, seasonings, brines, vinegars and oils— make a pungent addition to pasta salads. For best flavor, seek out good-quality cured olives, such as French Niçoise, Greek Kalamata or Italian Gaeta varieties.

To Pit an Olive: Use an olive pitter, which grips the olive and pushes out the pit in one squeeze. Or, carefully slit the olive lengthwise down to the pit with a small, sharp knife. Pry the flesh away from the pit; if the flesh sticks to the pit, carefully cut it away.

PEPPERS

The widely varied pepper family ranges in form and taste from large, mild bell peppers (capsicums) to small, spicy-hot chilies, and may be used as colorful main ingredients or lively accents in a wide range of pasta soups and salads.

Fresh, sweet-fleshed bell peppers are most common in the unripe green form, although ripened red or yellow varieties are also available. Creamy pale yellow, orange and purple-black types may also be found.

Red chilies are sold fresh and dried. Fresh green chilies include the mild-to-hot dark green poblano, which resembles a tapered, triangular bell pepper; the long, mild Anaheim, or New Mexican; and the smaller, fiery jalapeño and serrano. When handling any chilies, wear rubber gloves to prevent any cuts or abrasions on your hands from contacting the peppers' volatile oils; wash your hands well

1. Preheat a broiler (griller). Cut the bell peppers in half lengthwise and remove the stems, seeds and ribs as directed below.

2. Place the pepper halves on a broiler pan, cut-side down, and broil until the skins are evenly blackened.

3. Transfer the peppers to a paper or plastic bag, close it and let stand until the peppers soften and are cool to the touch, about 10 minutes.

4. Using your fingertips or a small knife, peel off the blackened skins. Then tear or cut the peppers as directed in the recipe.

with warm, soapy water and take special care not to touch your eyes or other sensitive areas.

To Seed and Derib Peppers: Cut the pepper in half lengthwise with a sharp knife. Pull out the stem section from each half, along with the cluster of seeds attached to it. Remove any remaining seeds, along with any thin white membranes, or ribs, to which they are attached.

REDUCE

To boil or briskly simmer a liquid until it partially evaporates, thus concentrating its flavor and thickening its consistency. The wider the diameter of the pan being used, the more quickly a liquid will reduce. Judge the degree to which a liquid has been reduced by noting its level on the side of the pan, or pour it into a heatproof glass measuring cup.

SHRIMP

Fresh, raw shrimp (prawns) are generally sold with the heads already removed but the shell intact.

To Peel and Devein Shrimp: Using your thumbs, split open the thin shell along the inner curve, between the two rows of legs. Peel away the shell, taking care—if the recipe calls for it—to leave the last segment with tail fin intact and attached to the meat. Using a small, sharp knife, carefully make a shallow slit along the outer curve, just deep enough to expose the long, usually dark, veinlike intestinal tract. With the tip of the knife or your fingers, lift up and pull out the vein and discard it.

TOMATOES

During summer, when tomatoes are in season, use the best red or yellow vine-ripened tomatoes you can find. At other times, plum, sometimes called

Basic Terms and Techniques

Roma, tomatoes have the best flavor and texture. Store fresh tomatoes of any kind in a cool, dark place. Refrigeration causes them to break down quickly. Use within a few days of purchase.

To Peel and Seed Tomatoes

1. Bring a saucepan of water to a boil. Using a small, sharp knife, cut out the core of the tomato. Cut a shallow X in the opposite end.

2. Submerge the tomato for about 10 seconds in the boiling water, then remove and dip in a bowl of cold water.

3. Starting at the X, peel the skin, using your fingertips and, if necessary, the knife blade. Cut the tomatoes in half crosswise.

4. To seed, hold the tomato upside down and squeeze it gently to force out the seed sacs.

BASIC RECIPES

Designed to be made ahead, stored and added to many of the dishes, these basic stock recipes provide fresh, preservative-free alternatives to similar commercial products.

VEGETABLE STOCK

Include onions, carrots and other root vegetables in this stock. Avoid broccoli, cauliflower and cabbages, which can overwhelm the herb flavors.

3 qt (3 l) water
12 cups (2½ lb/1.25 kg) cut-up vegetables
12 fresh parsley stems
3 fresh thyme sprigs
1 bay leaf

1. In a large pot over high heat, combine the water, vegetables, parsley, thyme and bay leaf. Bring to a boil.
2. Reduce the heat to low and simmer until the stock is fragrant and flavorful, 1–1½ hours. Periodically add water to the pot to maintain the original level.
3. Line a sieve or colander with cheesecloth (muslin) and strain the stock through it into a large bowl.
4. If not using immediately, store in a tightly covered container in the refrigerator for up to 3 days or in the freezer for up to 2 months.
Makes 3 qt (3 l)

CHICKEN STOCK

The best chicken stock is the one you make yourself. If you must substitute, use a low-salt, lowfat canned or frozen chicken broth.

3   qt (3 l) water
5   lb (2.5 kg) chicken parts, fat removed
1   onion, peeled and chopped
1   carrot, peeled and chopped
12 fresh parsley stems
1   teaspoon minced fresh or ½ teaspoon crumbled dried thyme
1   bay leaf

1. In a large pot over high heat, combine the water, chicken parts, onion, carrot, parsley, thyme and bay leaf. Bring to a boil.
2. Reduce the heat to low and simmer, uncovered, until the meat has fallen off the bones and the stock is fragrant and flavorful, 3–4 hours. Periodically add water to the pot to maintain the original level.
3. Line a sieve or colander with cheesecloth (muslin) and strain the stock through it into a large bowl. Cool, cover and refrigerate until a layer of fat solidifies on top. Remove and discard the hardened fat.
4. If not using immediately, store in a tightly covered container in the refrigerator for up to 3 days or in the freezer for up to 2 months.

Makes 3 qt (3 l)

FISH STOCK

The best bones for stock are snapper, grouper, cod, perch, sole, trout and pike. If you must substitute, use bottled clam juice.

2   lb (1 kg) fish bones
4   cups (32 fl oz/4 l) water
1   cup (8 fl oz/250 ml) dry white wine
1   small onion, peeled and chopped
1   small carrot, peeled and chopped
12 fresh parsley stems
1   teaspoon minced fresh or ½ teaspoon crumbled dried thyme
1   bay leaf

1. Remove the gills, fat, tail and any traces of blood from the fish bones. Wash the bones.
2. In a large pot over high heat, combine the fish bones, water, wine, onion, carrot, parsley stems, thyme and bay leaf. Bring to a boil.
3. Reduce the heat to low and simmer, uncovered, for 40 minutes. Using a wooden spoon, crush the bones.
4. Line a sieve or colander with cheesecloth (muslin) and strain the stock through it into a large bowl. Cool, cover and refrigerate until a layer of fat solidifies on top. Remove and discard the hardened fat.
5. If not using immediately, store in a tightly covered container in the refrigerator for up to 3 days or in the freezer for up to 2 months.

Makes 5 cups (40 fl oz/1.25 l)

Jndex